What readers have said:

Part whirlwind history, part sacred biography, part holy swash-buckler, Ray Wiseman tells a rollicking good story about how God wastes nothing: from exile to homecoming, through windfall and pitfall, by trial and serendipity, God can shape a man's heart after his own. In this case the man is Paul Chang, missionary and Kingdom ambassador. Now, thanks to *A Bridge to the Mountain*, Paul can take his rightful place with the great cloud of witnesses—those heroes who remind us that true greatness comes through child-like humility and warrior courage.

> Mark Buchanan, author of *Things Unseen: Living in Light of Forever*, and *The Holy Wild: Trusting in the Character of God.*

Outwardly the biography of one man, *A Bridge to the Mountain* relates the story of a ministry family that spans three generations. It portrays their struggles and their successes, their joys and their sorrows, their delights and their difficulties. While it reminds all of the rare privilege of serving the Lord, it also warns of the immense impact it can have on the families of God's servants. As a pastor and son of a pastor, I could resonate with many of the events and challenges the Chang family faced and endured.

> David Ralph, Lead Pastor, Lakeside Church, Guelph, Canada

A word from a co-worker:

A few people have the almost inexplicable gift of walking into peoples lives and causing a stir that puts them at risk of facing major change. Some folk respect such people as inspirational and a blessing while others label them as controlling and chaotic. Paul is one such person: he will draw you to him and engender love; or he will disturb you and cause you to keep your distance.

When Paul walked into my life as a total stranger ten years ago, he started a chain of events that totally changed my life. I eventually gave up my cardiology practice for the Lord's mission! That was an expensive encounter.

I respect the man for his vision even though many times he runs too far ahead for people to understand him. I respect him for his energy even though, like a tornado, he can sweep past people. I respect him for his fearlessness in the face of so many storms that would have drowned many lesser men. I respect him for his gentleness, for under this type-A character, dwells a beautiful sensitivity. I respect him for his wisdom, for out of the depth of his rich experience he gives counsel generously.

But above all, I respect him for his heart. Paul has a heart of gold. He cares and he gives fully of himself for the weakest and the poorest.

Paul is a man of God. He knows the Lord. He loves Him. He is faithful to His master. And God loves this tough little gem. Out of the hardest of struggles in life, his God has walked with him, moulded him, used him and cared for him every step of his way. Paul himself gladly sings of the "mercy and kindness of the Lord forever."

Such is Paul, my friend, my big brother, and indeed my mentor.

Thank you, Paul.

Dr. Ben Sia, Melbourne, Australia, August 2003

A Bridge to the Mountain

Fall 2003 Book Launch!
A Bridge to the Mountain

Paul Chang   Ray Wiseman

Dedicated to the memory of Chang Hsueh Kung and all other twentieth-century disciples and apostles who gave their lives for the sake of the gospel in China.

ALSO BY RAY WISEMAN:

I Cannot Dream Less

Aunt Harri Walks the Line

Disciples of Joy

A Difficult Passage

A Bridge to the Mountain
The life and ministry of Paul Chang

By Ray Wiseman

CNEC **Southeast Asia & Partners International—Canada**

Published jointly in 2003 by:

Partners International—Canada
8500 Torbram Road, Unit 56
Brampton, ON L6T 5C6
Canada

Christian Nationals Evangelism Commission (Southeast Asia)
134/136 Braddell Road
Singapore 359919

ISBN: 0-9698108-3-0

Printed in Canada.

AUTHOR'S PREFACE

When writing a book about cultures as diverse as East from West, authors meet many challenges that require thoughtful decisions. First they must attempt to cross the cultural gap, and then help the reader to span the divide. The following comments on structure and technique indicate how this author with the help of his editor faced these challenges.

Pinyin spelling: Generally, this book follows the Romanization system for writing the Chinese language developed by the government of the People's Republic of China. Known as Pinyin, it has some letters that have no relation to phonetics understood by English-speaking people. They appear below with approximate phonetic equivalents:

X = *sh*, as in Xidan
Q = *ch* as in Qing
C = *ts* as in Ci Xi, the dowager empress

In some places, because of familiarity, we have retained the older, or Wade-Giles form of spelling.

Names: Chinese names appear in the traditional way with the family name first, e.g., *Chang Bao-wha*. When a westernized Chinese name appears, it follows the Western format as in *Paul Chang.*

Cultural differences: Here we walk a narrow pathway, trying not to offend Chinese people while at the same time using a style that Westerners understand. This shows up in titles. In Southeast Asia, people typically refer to ordained ministers as *Reverend*, and write it informally as in Rev. Chang. They reserve the term *pastor* for non-ordained Christian workers—so they consider it a put-down to call an ordained minister Pastor. Formal English requires the full spelling of the title *Reverend* as in the *Reverend Paul Chang*. We have opted to follow the more commonly used and informal abbreviation, *Rev.*, as in *Rev. Paul Chang*. We have also chosen to use an informal or Western method of dealing with names by calling individuals by their family names at times and, at other times, by their given names. Depending on the context, we might refer to Paul Chang as: *Rev. Paul Chang, Dr. Paul Chang, Chang,* or *Paul.* Although in Chinese culture this might seem disrespectful, we intend none.

Point of view: Often the point of view in the narrative will change from that of the author to Paul Chang or another character. Such changes typically appear following minor section titles (introduced with bold face) or three centred asterisks (***).

Dialogue: To give life to the account we have often recreated dialogue. Conversations reflect the essence of what happened, if not the actual words. In one case, the story of Martha, we could not know the actual circumstances, so created a scenario that accurately portrays the horror of child slavery and prostitution.

Chronology: We have tried to keep events in chronological order but, in some circumstances where it aids in more simply telling the story, we have strayed from this rule.

CNEC/*Partners International:* The organization began as CNEC but later changed its name in parts of the world to Partners International. The United Kingdom uses the name WorldShare. Whether the book calls it CNEC, Partners International, or PI, it refers to the same organization.

TABLE OF CONTENTS

MAPS

ACKNOWLEDGEMENTS

Authors can't possibly thank all those who help them make their books possible. Like those who win movie Oscars, we would have to say, "I'd like to begin by thanking my mother and my English teacher . . ."

Personally, I would never get to the end!

Nevertheless, I will try. First mention goes to the Chang family: Paul, Nien-chang, Mark, and Ruth. They searched their memories and opened their hearts-surprising me often and themselves occasionally.

Then I must thank a great host of people associated with Partners International/CNEC. Folks who filled positions all the way from international director to sponsored child—from those just beginning to those retired for many years. Without the enthusiastic cooperation offered in at least ten countries by people from many nationalities, tribes, and cultures, the book could not have happened.

I will mention a few individuals who helped in special ways—with apologies to all those that space disallowed.

Thanks to:
- Anna Wiseman who proofread every word and helped in the original interviews and research;
- Mark Clayton who edited every thought and line and created the cover;
- Soh Ming Wah who searched the text for errors in fact and corrected my bad spelling of Chinese names; and
- Pauline Whyte who formatted the text in preparation for the printer.

I have left the most important acknowledgement to the last—thanks to Him who provided the health, energy, and finances to complete the task.

—Ray Wiseman, Fergus, Ontario.

FOREWORD

By the Reverend Dr. John Kao

It has been my great privilege and delight to read through the life story and missionary endeavours of the Reverend Dr. Paul Chang whom I have known as a good friend and co-worker for more than half of a century. I had heard many stories from this book in his talks on various occasions. It is amazingly interesting—especially to audiences with a western cultural background. The author adds much colourful imagery to make this biography lively and dramatic. He has done considerable research in specific areas of history that many readers will find helpful.

Paul and I encountered similar circumstances during the earlier years of our lives. I admire Paul's courage in the journey of faith and adventure and the wonderful protection and provision of our heavenly Father. During the early 1950s, Paul's positive attitude toward various facets of life appeared capricious to those around him—not serious enough in the face of life's difficulties. Praise the Lord that He furnished good opportunities for Paul to study in America. We were especially grateful to God when He provided Nien-chang as Paul's help-meet and encourager. As it is said, "Behind every great man there is a great woman." As friends, we often felt that Nien-chang deserved much more behind-the-scene credit as Paul's life story played out. After their marriage, their life appeared to have more steadfastness and focus on the work of the Lord.

Their talents in music have made them a perfect couple in deputational ministries. Their simple life style and willingness to relocate to different countries have contributed to their success in becoming an admirable missionary family. They have great compassion for poor and suffering people. Praise the Lord for the excellent influence of the Chang family in preaching the gospel and caring for the needy. Paul and Nien-chang have raised abundant support for the poverty stricken fields in Southeast Asia. Paul's pioneering spirit in developing various regions of national ministry is rare among his peers, our Chinese co-workers. I think the Reverend Allen and Ruth Finley deserve much credit as Paul and Nien-chang's mentors—and for developing other national Christian leaders.

During the earlier phase of his leadership in ministry, Paul did encounter much resistance and misunderstanding; it might well be that Paul himself, like his daughter Ruth, faced a certain degree of identity crisis. It might serve us all better if we took more of an incarnational approach in accommodating the native culture and exercised more interpersonal skills in dealing with co-workers.

Praise the Lord! He has come a long way toward maturity in Christian spirituality, leadership, and creativity in missionary services. Paul and Nien-chang's dedication and faithfulness in the unwavering ministry of CNEC/Partners International have won the admiration of our co-workers and Christian circle at large. I am greatly honoured to be a friend and co-worker of the Chang family.

I recommend this excellent book for all individuals and church libraries, for missionary education and encouragement, so that God would raise up more missionaries like the Chang family.

INTRODUCTION

To Western eyes, China appears merely as a shadow on the eastern horizon of history. Occidentals know it exists but can't quite see it beyond the clutter of their own great European empires, technological advances, and glorious civilizations.

Chinese people look to their western horizon and write off what they see as fractured societies and bankrupt cultures that have barely shrugged off the darkness of the Middle Ages. They look inward and see threads of a great civilization spanning thousands of years of history, culture, and arts, often interrupted, sometimes influenced, but never broken by changing dynasties, invasions, and other contacts with the rest of the world.

The ancient concept of China as the centre of the world still has validity today in the minds of modern Chinese people.

When I visited China in 1994, I had no idea I would one day write a book against the backdrop of Chinese history and culture. Like most westerners, I had a distorted view of China. But we all have much to learn and modern China handed me a few surprises. I wrote the following, published in the *Guelph Mercury* in March of that year.

***

CUI HENG, CHINA: I fully expected China to look dreary and drab, its people dull, humourless, and committed to the party line, and its industry outdated and primitive. What else could one expect after a half century of Communism? But not everything fitted my preconceptions.

The buildings, roads, and countryside, all seemed painted by one brush dipped in one colour, a dull pale brown. I might have been looking at China in a collection of old sepia photographs. I mentally checked off my first expectation. Yes, China looks dreary and drab.

The Chinese tour guide seemed a little disappointed that only a few of the Canadians on the bus had heard of Sun Yat-sen. She said, "We are approaching the village of Cui Heng, the birthplace of the founder of modern China. Sun Yat-sen over-threw the Manchurian emperors and founded the first Chinese republic in 1912."

"I am sure you have all heard of Chiang Kai-shek," she continued. "They were brothers-in-law. But Sun Yat-sen had a rather different view of China. Chiang would have returned us to a monarchy. That is why the Chinese people rejected him."

I smiled as the guide echoed the party or government line. For the most part she had seemed unbiased and open as she discussed the accomplishments and problems of the People's Republic of China. She had joked about our physical differences as we approached the border of a special economic area. "People need a special permit to live or visit this area," she said. "They check each person who goes through for the right papers. But they won't bother us. They will see the big eyes and big noses and wave us through."

In fact they did enter our bus long enough to check the passports of the two young ladies from Hong Kong who travelled with us. As we pulled away, the guide said, "Sometimes, they make a mistake and pull over Japanese tourists. You can tell the difference between Chinese and Japanese can't you?"

When none of us answered, she placed her fingers at the outer edges of her eyes and began distorting their shape, saying, "Chinese eyes slope down like this, but Japanese eyes slope upward like this. Sometimes Japanese tourists wear sun glasses, but you can still recognize them. You know how don't you?" Again we disappointed her with our ignorance. Shaking her head and waving her finger she said, "By their cameras!"

I remembered my second expectation: Chinese people are dull, humourless, and committed to the party line. Wrong there; none of the people I met, and certainly not this tour guide, fitted that description.

Our Mitsubishi bus bumped and vibrated as we sped down a modern multi-lane highway. However, the problem originated with the road, not the bus. The concrete surface didn't have the mirror-like finish we expect in Canada. I guessed they had built it with light equipment and hand labour. Our bus swung wide to pass a row of mini-trucks, each one loaded with building materials. The power plants looked like garden tractors, the kind you walk behind and steer with long handlebars—except that they pulled trailers. The driver sat on the front of the trailer and gripped the handlebars to control the vehicle. I thought: *Those things are modern versions of the age-old ox cart.*

Our guide interrupted my thoughts: "Coming up next you will see modern factories. We have attracted a number of international companies to begin joint ventures in this special economic zone. You might think of this area as the Silicon Valley of China." I saw modern factories, some displaying the names of well-known Japanese electronics firms. The sepia look had vanished; it could have been an industrial subdivision anywhere in the world. Well, almost anywhere—the bumpy road reminded me we had not left China.

My third expectation, that China depended on outdated and primitive industry, had proven partly right, but mostly wrong. I saw China emerging from the past and racing toward the future. I have a strong feeling all of us will become much more aware of China in the next few years.

***

Since writing that piece and having begun a study of China, its people, and the life of the Reverend Dr. Paul Chang (born Chang Bao-wha), I have received many more surprises. I trust that you too will experience the same sense of wonder as you enter the orient through the pages of this book.

Paul Chang's route to safety

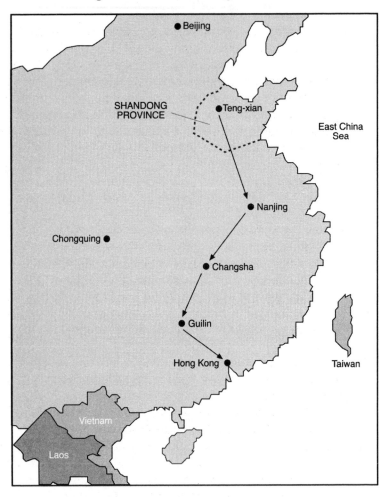

PROLOGUE

What you do not want done to yourself, do not do unto others.
The injuries done to you by an enemy should be returned
with a combination of love and justice.

So said Kung Fu Tzu,[1] China's most revered teacher and
philosopher. He envisioned a land where everyone sought to
live a good life, where morality would flow upward from the
family through society to the nation's leaders who would rule
with justice, and all would live in harmony.

It didn't turn out that way.

***

Six-year-old Bao-wha walked the inside perimeter of his
narrowed world. He wanted to leave the compound and race
freely along paths that led through the fields to friends' houses.
He yearned to climb trees looking for birds' nests, catch
grasshoppers, and collect papers to sell to the paper mill. He
could still play football with friends who lived within the walls,
but he yearned to escape the bricks and mortar that had become
his prison.

However, he dared not leave the grounds of the seminary
since the day his father, Chang Hsueh Kung, had forbidden all
trips beyond the wall.

"The Japanese Imperial Army now rules our province," his
father had said. "They have done unspeakable things to Chinese
people. Leaving the compound would put you in extreme
danger. For now we are safe within the walls."

Bao-wha wrestled with concepts that no child should ever
face. The Japanese had invaded and ravaged the countryside
around his home in Teng-xian, northern China. Because the
Chang family lived within the walls of the Northern China
Theological Seminary, the invaders had stopped short of their
home, but not due to respect for religious institutions. They
hesitated because an American flag flew at the gate and several

American missionary families lived within the compound. The Japanese did not yet wish to provoke the United States to enter the war.

During his solitary walk, Bao-wha approached the church. Slipping inside for a few moments, he felt the cool floor on his bare feet, but a touch of warmth burned within. Was God present here in the same way he had lived in the Tabernacle? He liked to think the Japanese soldiers could see a pillar of fire above the church and dare not enter the grounds for fear God would strike them dead. He liked to believe God, not the American flag, kept the invaders beyond the walls.

Outside again, he walked by the seminary dormitories and continued on until he reached the family home. A twinge of resentment shot through his body. Strangers now occupied it, filling every room, preparing food in his mother's kitchen, and sleeping in his bedroom. Father had given away their house.

"Refugees," Father had said, "here they will find safety from the Japanese. We can move into the second floor of the dormitory."

They had done exactly that, but even as they moved into their new quarters, Father had issued another warning. "We must use even more care since giving sanctuary to the refugees. The enemy will seek other ways to threaten or intimidate us."

Bao-wha now turned back toward the dormitory. The growing sound of hundreds of footsteps filled the air. He paused to listen, but when he heard strange words spoken in Japanese, he raced for the dormitory. His short legs became a blur of energy as he shot up the stairs, past the rooms where he now lived, and up a ladder into the attic.

Dropping to his knees, he pushed the shutter open. From here he could see over the west wall to the railway tracks that skirted the seminary on that side. From an attic window, Bao-wha watched as soldiers of the Japanese Imperial army marched hundreds of Chinese people along the railway track and crowded them together like a herd of human animals.

"What are they doing?" the boy wondered. "Is this a parade? Are they going on a picnic?"

In a moment he knew. The murderous clatter of machine-gun fire echoed off the seminary walls and buildings. People fell like small trees before a bulldozer. Within a minute hundreds lay dead and dying on the tracks. A few, still living, sought safety beneath the bodies of fallen comrades.

Gun smoke drifted over the wall; its acrid smell reached the attic. While Bao-wha watched, soldiers stacked the bodies and doused them with gasoline. They drew back and hurled a torch into the pile of rejected humanity. Even as the flames exploded skyward, the child saw isolated arms and legs move as if attempting a last-minute escape.

The foul smell of burning flesh accosted Bao-wha's nose and lungs as the inferno turned the dead, dying, and hiding into a charred mound.

***

Three thousand years of Chinese history had suddenly converged on one small boy. For centuries foreign armies had invaded and raped the Chinese countryside, driving the common people into hiding—making them refugees in their own land—wantonly killing innocent people, destroying farms, and pillaging factories. The Japanese army, as though in a frenzy to repeat history, would soon breach the fragile protection of a foreign flag and desecrate the church within the wall. Before Bao-wha could grow up, other armies would follow, driving his family southward, and crushing the symbols and remnants of Christianity in its wake.

Is China forever destined to repeat the cycles of peace and invasion? Of good government followed by rebellion? Of Christian penetration succeeded by utter expulsion?

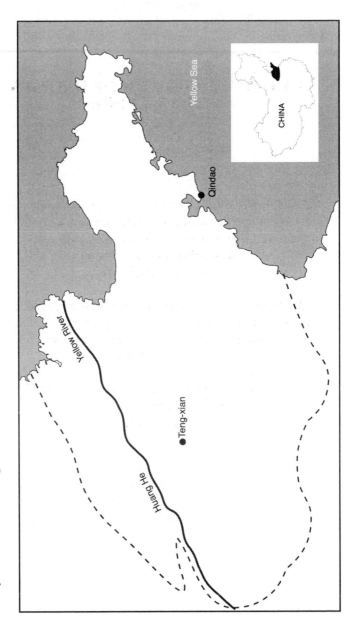

Map of Shandong Province, China

PART 1: THE POWER OF HISTORY AND CULTURE

There is nothing that strengthens a nation like reading of a nation's own history, whether its history is recorded in books or embodied in customs, institutions and monuments.
—Joseph Anderson

Men commonly think according to their inclinations, speak according to their learning and imbibed opinions, but generally act according to custom.
—Francis Bacon

For everything that was written in the past was written to teach us . . .
—Romans 15:4

CHAPTER 1 : *Links to the Past*

The Bible says, "In the beginning God created the heavens and the earth² . . .," and, "In the beginning was the Word and the Word was God."³

And so the life story of any man truly begins—not with a childhood adventure—but in the remote historical and cultural dawn of his nation. To fully understand Paul Chang, born Chang Bao-wha, we must go back, way back . . .

***

According to Chinese folklore, the Chinese people originated in the Huang He valley.⁴ In their tradition the world and mankind came about through the creative actions of one who appeared as God and man merged into one being. Legend tells us P'an Ku (Pan Gu) broke free from embryonic chaos, appearing from an egg as a creature with two horns, two tusks, and a hairy body. Some versions say he separated heaven and earth, divided the four seas, put sun, moon and stars in place, and chiselled out mountains and valleys to shape the world. Mythology claims that a series of heavenly, terrestrial, and human sovereigns succeeded him.

Archaeological evidence indicates the people grew rice in eastern China about 5500 BC and, about five centuries later, an agricultural society developed in the Huang He valley. Strong evidence exists to support two so-called pottery cultures, the Yang-shao culture (4000–1700 BC), and the Lung-shan culture (2000–1850 BC).

Sometime after 1100 BC during the Zhou Dynasty,⁵ the "mandate of heaven" emerged—a political concept that teaches heaven gives a mandate to rule to wise and virtuous leaders. Under this doctrine, the emperor became known as the Son of Heaven. In time the concept expanded to include the Taoist theory that heaven disapproves bad rulers through natural disasters such as floods, earthquakes, and plagues. It also allowed for rebellion by the people against tyrannical rulers and for the rebel leaders to claim the mandate of heaven to rule in place of the deposed emperor.

This gave rise to the "dynastic cycle," which maintains that when the moral quality of the ruling family erodes, heaven will pass power on to others. Hence an endless cycle began in which dynasties rose, prospered, became corrupt, and then gave way to new, just rulers.

At this time the Chinese also developed the concept of a separate identity. Even when divided into separate kingdoms they maintained a belief in the superiority of their culture. They identified as barbarians all those who lived beyond their borders.

Let us from the West remember that we—always ready to judge others—also have problems with ethnocentricity and have believed in such doctrines as "the divine right of kings"[6] and "manifest destiny."[7]

The dynastic cycle
The cycle continued for centuries, at times with a nation consolidated politically, and at times with smaller states vying for domination, but always with a strong sense of cultural unity. Outsiders, both friendly and hostile, entered the land. Missionaries of various religions and traders from afar came to find a welcome under one dynasty only to face expulsion under another. Invaders from the north strove for domination and sometimes succeeded in gaining power and placing their stamp on Chinese history.

The Mongols under Genghis Khan began a Chinese invasion in AD 1211, but succeeded only after 60 years under the leadership of Genghi's grandson, Kublai Khan. The Mongols ruled for only a century, but left a permanent mark on Chinese history. They improved the roads linking Russia and China, promoted trade with Europe, expanded the canal system, and instituted a famine-relief program.

China returned to Chinese rule during the Ming period, but fell again to northerners, the Manchus, who set up the Qing Dynasty.

The Manchus began as the Jurched tribe who lived in Manchuria just north of Korea. Although they became a strong force in Manchuria, they fell under Mongol control. During the Ming period they embraced Chinese culture, eating habits, and living customs. They rapidly abandoned their nomadic cultural tradition when the Chinese taught them how to build forts and farms. They quite remarkably traversed several hundred years of development in a short time and, under strong leadership, conquered China. The Chinese had unwittingly nurtured and trained those who, although not Chinese, became the last dynasty, lasting from 1644 to 1911. However, the Manchus— much more than the Mongols before them—did their best to further adopt Chinese culture and philosophy.

Under them the arts flourished and culture bloomed. However, in attempting to emulate the Chinese, they became conservative and inflexible. In their approach to foreign affairs, they insisted that everyone treat the emperor like the Son of Heaven and not recognize other countries as China's equal. This created great tensions with representatives of the West who now came on the scene in a big way.

China thrust onto the world stage
Western nations, notably, England, Russia, Germany, France, and the United States, tried to establish relations with China, but initially failed. The Manchus had no room in their ethnocentric world view for equality of nations. They saw China as central and the rest of the world as secondary. This viewpoint hindered Chinese reformers who found themselves accused of being westerners with Chinese faces.

This arrogant attitude of the Manchu rulers must have frustrated westerners who arrived with an equally exaggerated view of the supremacy of their own culture and achievements.

The Portuguese led the western encroachments in 1515 and received permission to establish a base in Macau in 1557. In the following century the British, Dutch, and Spanish arrived. The Manchu government initially rebuffed the European traders, but eventually opened the port of Canton for foreign trade in 1685.

When the balance of trade heavily favoured China, the Europeans looked for ways to turn it around.

The British found the answer. In 1773 they began selling Indian opium to the Chinese. When opium addiction became a serious problem the emperor banned it, but the British traders and corrupt Chinese officials and businessmen defied the ban. Tensions between Europeans and Chinese erupted into an invasion of Canton by the British, resulting in the first "Opium War"—three more wars followed, involving British, French, Americans, and Russians.

A series of unequal treaties to end the opium wars resulted in costly reparations for China, while western powers gained control of many ports. They also won the right to settle in specific areas and travel freely in China with immunity from Chinese law.

The nations that had fought to continue the illegal opium trade—a business that brought destruction to millions in China—now began to send Christian missionaries.

While many European nations gained control of parts of China, the British became de facto rulers and opened the door to missions. Peter Stursberg observes:

> China, although not formally part of the Empire, was the greatest prize. Certainly, the Christian churches regarded it as such: they mounted the largest campaign ever, sending thousands of missionaries, more than ten thousand at one time, to spread the Gospel among the Chinese, convert them, and bring the most populous country into Christendom. It was to be the last Crusade.[8]

The Manchu government, while claiming the high ground in its battle against the opium trade, had problems of its own. Rampant corruption, a steady decentralization of power, and the loss of control on many fronts plagued them. Rebellions and apocalyptic cults frustrated what little government authority remained. Squabbling between various reformers, who disagreed on how to oppose the internal chaos and the incursions of the

West, only made things worse. Two events, the Taiping and Boxer rebellions, almost toppled them.

The Taiping rebellion

Hung Xiuquan, the son of a poor farmer near Canton, repeatedly failed the civil service examination in Canton. Following one failure, he met a Christian missionary and received some Christian literature. The next year, after failing another exam, he had several visions that he interpreted as messages from God. He saw himself as the younger brother of Jesus Christ and sent by God to earth to eradicate demons and demon worship.

He did not act on his vision until seven years later following study with a Southern Baptist minister, Issachar J. Roberts. Roberts taught him everything he would know about Christianity. Hung, aided by relatives and followers, formed a new religious sect, dedicated to destroying idols in the Canton area. They organized in military fashion and began to build up a treasury and a store of weapons.

Hung's movement became an open revolt when government forces attacked it in 1850. Hung declared that God had established a new kingdom, the Kingdom of Heavenly Peace; he styled himself as Heavenly King—the era of the Taiping or 'Great Peace' had begun. Hung saw the Heavenly Kingdom bringing peace and prosperity to China with all people worshipping the one and only true God.

Hung espoused radical economic reform with all wealth equally distributed throughout a society that would have no class distinctions. He saw women as social and economic equals with men. The new order would return China to its legendary roots in which the common people owned and tilled the land collectively. It would outlaw slavery, plural and arranged marriages, tobacco, alcohol, foot binding, the opium trade, and idol worship. With its high ideals, passionate anti-Manchu nationalism, and social and economic reform, the Kingdom of Heavenly Peace drew multitudes of Chinese people suffering from the disasters and upheavals of the time.

Hung took control of large areas of south and central China, including the southern capital of Nanjing where he established a theocratic-military government. Excluding its Christian roots, the Heavenly Kingdom in many ways foreshadowed the later communist movement. It failed when the Western nations supported the Manchu government.

With the aid of the Western powers, the Manchus counterattacked, driving the Taipings into Nanjing. Bolstered by British army regulars and European and American mercenaries, the Manchus captured Nanjing and slaughtered the defenders. Hung Xiuquan committed suicide, thus ending the short-lived Kingdom of Heavenly Peace.

The Boxer rebellion
Throughout the 1800s foreigners encroached further and further into China, forcing the Manchu government to make humiliating concessions. Foreign regiments, armed with modern weapons, regularly defeated imperial armies. Great Britain, France, Germany, Japan, and Russia, among others divided China into "spheres of influence"—areas in which they claimed exclusive trading rights. The United States also vied for access to Chinese markets, having recently become an Asian power by acquiring the Philippines.

Ci Xi, the empress dowager of the Manchu or Qing Dynasty, searched for ways to rid the empire of foreign parasites. She thought she had an answer in a secret society called the Righteous and Harmonious Fists—the Boxers.

In northern Shandong province, a devastating drought had pushed people to the edge of starvation. There the Boxers had attracted thousands of followers. They developed a form of physical and spiritual training aimed at harmonizing mind and body in order to prepare for combat. They believed their rituals would cause spirits to possess their bodies and make them immune to the foreign bullets of the enemy. They also taught that millions of "spirit soldiers" would rise from the dead and join their cause.

Initially, they intended to overthrow the imperial government and expel all foreigners from the land. The crafty empress, however, with no better way to combat the foreign intruders, decided to encourage them. A new slogan appeared on the Boxers' banner—"Support the Qing; destroy the foreigner!"

Between 1898–1899 the Boxers began attacking Chinese Christians, but soon began killing British missionaries. In the spring of 1900 the Boxers were out of control, massacring Chinese Christians, missionaries, and other foreigners, and fomenting riots around Peking. The Europeans and Americans sent in troops who fought both Boxers and government troops, soon putting down the rebellion.

The foreign powers punished China with executions of government officials and Boxer leaders and exacted huge reparations, but they did not break up the Chinese nation. An empire at least outwardly unified suited their purposes—the lucrative opium trade could continue.

Although the Manchu reign continued for a few years, secret societies bent on bringing it down flourished, and the country descended into turmoil. The empress died in 1908. Provincial leaders opposed reforms and began supporting a coalition of rebel groups led by a Cantonese, Dr. Sun Yat-sen.

The modern republics
The First Republic, 1911–1949. During World War I, the Chinese Government sided with the Allies who, true to their historical involvement, betrayed China by handing over the German Concessions in Shangdong province to Japan.[9]

In the early 1920s, Dr. Sun Yat-sen, as the leader of the (up-to-then unsuccessful) Nationalist Party, accepted Soviet aid and forged an alliance with the fledgling Chinese Communist Party. They began the task of reunifying a China overrun with warlords. In 1925 Sun died of cancer and the leadership of the Nationalists, after a series of intrigues, went to Chiang Kai-shek.

The Nationalists almost immediately launched the "Northern Expedition" which took them from Guangzhou to Shanghai. With southern China now unified, they controlled the Lower Yangzi. In Shanghai, Chiang launched a communist massacre—he had previously had little use for them. A young communist named Mao Zedong managed to escape the carnage.

The Communists fled to the countryside where the Nationalists tried to hunt them down and, in the words of Chiang, "eliminate the cancer of Communism." In 1934, under the cover of night the Communists broke out and started running—a murderous trek that lasted a year. The Long March covered ten thousand km. Only four to eight thousand of the original one hundred thousand marchers arrived in northern China. Mao soon became sole leader of the Communists.

During this time the Japanese began occupying Manchuria. Chiang diverted his forces to fight the Japanese giving the Communists a respite. In 1937, the Japanese invaded China proper from their foothold in Manchuria and soon occupied the major coastal cities. In their own brand of ethnic cleansing, they burned bodies of multitudes of machine-gunned Chinese civilians. Estimates of the dead at the hands of the Japanese range above 20 million.[10]

Japan's entry into World War II turned their war effort away from fighting the Chinese toward the Americans. The Communists now strengthened their hold on northern China and prepared to face the Nationalists. In contrast to the Communists, disorganization and corruption plagued the Nationalists.

By 1949 uncontrollable corruption and debt crippled the Nationalists. They printed more money to pay their debts, which lead to excessive inflation. They fled to Taiwan and Mao Zedong proclaimed the creation of the People's Republic of China.

Oddly, the Communists didn't bother to reclaim for China either Macau or Hong Kong, even though Portugal and Britain could not have effectively protested.

The People's Republic of China: The new regime began in bankruptcy—Chiang had fled to Taiwan with the nation's gold reserves. The country's infrastructure, industrial production, and agricultural output had collapsed. Buoyed by victory in the Korean War and fear of attack by Western nations, China made tremendous advances. By 1953 they had halted inflation, restored production to pre-war levels, and confiscated land from landholders for redistribution to the peasants.

The government, as had many Chinese regimes before it, viewed Christianity as a Western religion and tried to eradicate it. They ejected missionaries and directed hostility toward Christians who lost their jobs, went to jail, or found themselves in labour camps.

In 1958, Mao, in an attempt to quickly transform the country into a developed nation, launched the "Great Leap Forward." His plan would create collective farms to increase crop production. Peasants not required in agriculture would work in small-scale industries and assist with rebuilding the nation's infrastructure. Having previously won their land, peasants now had to surrender it to the government.

The plan proved disastrous. Agricultural production fell and floods and droughts ruined the harvests, initiating one of the worst famines in history—millions died. To cap it off, in 1960 the Soviets withdrew all aid.

During the next few years conditions improved. A new period began with a shift away from collective farms to family ownership of farms and limited free markets. The power had begun to shift away from Mao—he found himself eclipsed by other political forces and blamed for the disasters of the Great Leap Forward. Mao may have believed the people had lost the spirit of revolution and had begun a slide back to capitalism. We can't know for certain what he thought, but in response, he launched the "Cultural Revolution."

Mao called students to rebel against authority and purge society of all human and physical reminders of the nation's past. They formed units of Red Guards and attacked writers, artists, and intellectuals. They destroyed their works and sent them to do physical labour in the countryside. China collapsed into anarchy. Universities and secondary schools closed. The Red Guards forced the end of cultural activities and publications, closed offices, and disrupted transportation. China had lapsed into a time equally as bad as any in her long history.

Once again, saner heads prevailed and the Cultural Revolution officially ended in 1969 along with its worst abuses—but tensions remained for a few years until Mao's death. Deng Xiaoping emerged as the pre-eminent leader in 1978 and immediately began an economic reform program. Deng's reforms began with agriculture but gradually spread to the rest of society.

Peter Stursberg interpreted the excesses in the uprisings of the last century with these words:

> It was the pent-up emotions of years of humiliation and shame that drove them to acts of destruction. The debacle of the Opium Wars and subsequent colonial subjugation, the rape and plunder of the country by British and other imperial forces, were a deeply held part of the collective subconscious.[11]

China continues to stagger toward a more open society, but the fits and starts so common in its history, seem to have diminished.

CHAPTER 2 : *China's Lost Churches*

*Jesus said to the apostles, "You will be my witnesses in
Jerusalem, and in all Judea and Samaria,
and to the ends of the earth."*[12]

Approximately 20 years after Jesus' challenge to the apostles,
one of them trekked eastward to India.[13] Did others continue on
to carry the Christian torch into China? Even in those days,
China did not quite mark the end of the world, for the East and
West knew of the existence of each other. For centuries before
Christ, tiny lateen-sailed and oar-driven vessels had crept from
headland to headland seeking trade and adventure and dissemi-
nating knowledge, however imperfect.

Timothy I, patriarch of the Nestorians wrote that the Magi
had returned to the East following their visit to Bethlehem and
introduced Christianity to lands east of the Euphrates. Nestorian
tradition also claims that Saint Thaddeus and Saint Maria, commissioned by Jesus from among the "seventy" to go to Asia,
brought the gospel to Edessa in the first century. This launched
the Nestorian or Syriac church that soon began reaching out to
neighbouring lands bordering on China.[14]

Although memories of Christianity's first forage into India
have adhered to its land and collective memory, nothing
remains to mark a similar visit to China. Does this mean early
Christians did not reach China? Not necessarily, for that great
land has a history of driving out the memory of Christian beach-
heads within its perimeters—as it did the Nestorian church.

The Nestorians
The Nestorian faith continued to grow eastward along the Silk
Roads that became a centre of commercial and cultural exchange,
bringing together merchants from most regions of Asia.

Converts to Nestorian Christianity from among traders
played a key role in spreading the faith eastward. In the 400s,
the Nestorians became theological cast offs due to a disagreement
with the rest of the church, believing Jesus' nature consisted of

two persons (rather than one person with two natures). At the same time the Nestorians rejected the concept of referring to Mary as "the Mother of God." Following their condemnation at the Council of Chalcedon in AD 451, they retained their missionary zeal, continuing their eastern thrust.

In AD 635 the Nestorian church sent missionaries via the silk trade route to spread the faith in China's northwest. The reigning emperor welcomed the Nestorian bishop, Alopen, allowed the newcomers to establish a monastery, requested that they translate the Christian scriptures into Chinese, and granted space in the imperial library for the task. Within decades, the Nestorian faith won thousands of converts in several major cities. The early Tang rulers, not themselves of pure Chinese extraction, supported religious diversity feeling it added legitimacy to their rule. They gave similar support to other non-Chinese faiths such as Buddhism.

For two centuries the Nestorians flourished under the blessing of the government but, in a blaze of national and cultural pride, Emperor Wu Tsung initiated a severe persecution against all foreign religions. He destroyed thousands of Buddhist monasteries, scattered the monks, and seized the land—a blow from which the Buddhists never recovered. The Nestorians fared no better; they essentially vanished from China proper, though not from the tribes of Turks and Mongols immediately to the north.

The great losses for the Nestorians and other foreign religions translates into a victory for the followers of Confucius who had promoted the persecution in order to remove the powers they had lost and to replenish the royal coffers with the wealth and land seized. Confucian temples appeared for the first time: the Chinese moral philosophy began taking on the trappings of a religion.

The Nestorians had failed to identify closely enough with Chinese culture and so had remained foreign, rather than becoming a national movement.[15]

The Church of the West comes East
In the late 1200s Genoese traders, members of the Polo family

arrived at the court of Kublai Khan, the Mongol ruler of China. Although their prime purpose was not evangelism, they did not hesitate to identify themselves as Christians. By this time the Nestorians had begun to reestablish themselves in China—the Mongol rulers filled key administrative positions with other Mongols, many of whom were Nestorian Christians. Very little communication existed between the Nestorian church and the Roman church, so the emperor's curiosity would draw him to Western Christians. In fact, the Polos so intrigued the ruler, that he sent them back to Rome with an invitation for the Pope to send 100 teachers of science and religion who must be "Intelligent men acquainted with the Seven Arts, able to enter into controversy, and able clearly to prove to idolaters and other kinds of folk that the law of Christ was best."[16]

This did not happen for another 20 years, when John of Monte Corvino, a Franciscan, arrived. Kublai Khan's successor warmly received him. One has to believe some form of pre-evangelism had taken place, for in quick time he baptized six thousand Chinese, established churches in several cities, and translated the New Testament and Psalms. He managed to continue his work despite criticism from high-ranking Nestorians who accused him of heresy and criminal activity. The Roman church in turn accused the eastern Christians of heresy.

Much of the success of the Roman missionaries had more to do with politics than religion. The Mongol rulers had entered into intrigues with the Pope to build an alliance between the East and the West against the increasing power of the Muslims.

When the Ming Dynasty replaced the Mongols in 1368, according to some estimates, China had as many as one hundred thousand Roman Catholic Christians. Persecution arrived with the Ming Dynasty. By the late 1500s history had repeated itself—Christians of both faiths again disappeared from China.

The Jesuits

In 1583 the Society of Jesus, commonly known as the Jesuits, entered China through the Portuguese colony of Macau. Under the leadership of Matteo Ricci, they elected a strategy to identify with the elites or opinion leaders of society. They dressed in the manner of Confucian scholars and carefully observed Chinese cultural customs. "(Ricci) adopted the terms used by Confucius to denote the Supreme Being in order to make real to the Chinese the Christian idea of God."[17]

Of their methods, Ralph R. Covell says:

> They prepared maps, practiced astronomy, constructed and repaired clocks they gave to the emperor, and they wrote treatises that explained Christianity in terms of a Confucian world view. The missionaries needed to be deliberately ostentatious about their learning to convince the Chinese of their expertise in European learning, so they would emboss their European books with gold covers.[18]

Franciscan and Dominican missionaries soon followed the Jesuits. However, they criticized the Jesuits for compromising the faith when they observed their accommodating approach to Chinese culture and Confucianism. Despite the tensions between Jesuits and others, by the beginning of the 1700s, the Roman Catholic church in China numbered two hundred thousand believers among scholars, city dwellers, and peasants.

During this time missionary enterprise became increasingly identified with colonialism. To evangelize meant the spreading of European Christian culture and European political power.

The differences and intrigues finally boiled over, involving the Vatican and the emperors. Controversy continued until 1724 when the emperor banned the Christian faith in China. Alternating periods of persecution followed until the early 1800s, during which time many missionaries suffered imprisonment, expulsion, and martyrdom.

Protestants Arrive
The establishment of the London Missionary Society in 1795 as a non-denominational body dedicated to world evangelism launched a century and a half of intensive missionary activity in

China. The American Board of Commissioners for Foreign Missions appeared in 1810 followed by a multitude of other inter-denominational and denominational groups.

Robert Morrison of the London Missionary Society, the first protestant missionary to China, arrived at Canton in 1807. He supported himself by working for the East India Company in a position that allowed him close contact with Chinese people. He translated most of the Bible into Chinese, wrote the first Chinese-English dictionary, published many gospel tracts, introduced Western medicine, and promoted education.

From the mid-1800s, treaties forced on the Chinese by Western nations to enhance trade—and particularly to keep opium traffic moving—also benefited missionaries. By 1869 the missionary force in China boasted 400 missionaries from over 30 denominations and by 1900 the number had grown to 2,800.

To a great extent the earlier concept of spreading European Christian culture as a component of the faith still prevailed throughout that century. Between 1860 and 1900, missionaries had established themselves in every province of China. During the Boxer rebellion, many missionaries died and most fled from their stations. But following the rebellion, missionaries received even greater rights. A treaty provided that mission societies could purchase property for mission purposes. This resulted in later accusations of foreign control of Christian work by foreigners. By 1907 most missionaries had returned to their stations; in that year protestant missionary societies reported 180,000 Chinese church members, not including children.

The main problem with missionaries of the time was their failure to appreciate Chinese cultural values: they tended to see everything Chinese as idolatrous while they saw Christianity and Western culture as inseparable.

"One of the most influential writers in Europe of this period maintained that the strength of Christianity was due to its inner vitality and to the powers within Western culture which gave dynamic to the Western world and its religion."[19]

The actions of the Western powers in supporting the illegal opium trade brought embarrassment to the missionaries and confusion to the Chinese. How could westerners harmonize their illegal activities with the clear teaching of the gospel? But despite opposition, the opium trade, and faulty missiology, missionaries influenced Chinese culture in a major way. They introduced Western-style education—including education for women—and established modern medical hospitals. Published figures for 1920 show a protestant, foreign mission force of 6,204 workers and a Chinese church with a total Christian constituency of 806,926 people from among a total population of 438,925,833.[20]

The political upheavals within China from 1900 to 1950, placed extra burdens on missionary societies, but they continued their work, often with excellent results—the numbers of foreign missionaries and Chinese Christians continued to increase.

In 1919 the Presbyterian Church of the United States established the Northern China Theological Seminary (NCTS). In the late 1920s, they identified a potential leader, Chang Hsueh Kung, and sponsored his attendance at Princeton Theological Seminary and the Moody Bible Institute. He returned to teach at NCTS and later became vice-principal and then principal. In 1932 he and his wife Liang Hui Ting had a son, Chang Bao-wha, better known by his Western name Paul Chang.

CHAPTER 3 : *Things of Mind and Spirit*

*Confucius said, "Enliven the ancient and also know
what is new; then you can be a teacher."*

In the 11th century BC, the Shang Dynasty gave way to the
Zhou, which introduced an era of advancement in politics,
technology, arts, and communications. Change brought with it
upheaval, which introduced the period of the warring states,
known also as China's classical age.

Confucianism

During this time, Chinese speculative thought flowered. Kung
Fu Tzu, known in English as Confucius, stands out as the key
thinker who has influenced Chinese culture to the present time.
Born in Shandong[21] province in 551 BC,[22] Confucius never
intended his teachings as a religion. He left no sacred writings,
founded no priesthood, or proclaimed no doctrine of an
afterlife. He even frowned on asceticism and monasticism. His
writings dealt fundamentally with personal morality and ethics
and the proper application of political power by the rulers.

Others later added religious embellishments, deifying him
by offering animal sacrifices at his tomb. Taoists and Buddhists
have blended Confucian ethics and moral teachings with their
religious concepts.

Confucius proposed two main social classes: 1) the peasants
who produced agricultural products, provided soldiers, and
worked as day-labourers for the state in lieu of taxes; and
2) an elite but small group of intellectuals and administrators.
Merchants, artisans, and military formed a third group,
grudgingly tolerated by the elite. The elite formed an alliance
with the emperor who controlled the military, police, and other
societal regulators. For the state to function, the groups needed
each other.

Confucius placed a major emphasis on character development and purity of heart and conduct. He taught that people
should first develop good character, which he considered the

best of all virtues. He saw all men as fundamentally good; he
believed they could observe goodness in the sages or teachers of
the nation. He described those who attained goodness as prince-
ly or virtuous men. Those who did not, he characterized as infe-
rior men clinging to material comfort and looking for rewards
and favours. He taught that the one is just, dignified, noble,
magnanimous, and humble; the other expects rewards and
favours and is mean, proud, crooked, and arrogant.

Confucius' main theme centred on the establishment and
continuance of good government. He said, "The Ruler himself
should be virtuous, just, honest and dutiful. A virtuous ruler is
like the Pole-star which, by keeping its place, makes all other
stars to revolve round it. As is the Ruler, so will be the   subjects."[23]

By the sixth century AD temples to honour Confucius
appeared in every prefecture in China.

In 1503 the emperor curbed the Confucian cult by ordering
the replacement of Confucius' images in the temples with
wooden tablets inscribed with his teachings.

Taoism

Lao-tze, which means *old philosopher* or *old boy*, founded
Taoism, in 604 BC in China. His real name was Li-uhr.
Confucius studied under Lao-tze. Taoism and Confucianism
complement each other: Taoism speaks chiefly of the unseen
and intangible, while Confucianism deals with moral issues,
proclaiming a system of moral precepts rather than religious
dogmas. Taoism concerns itself with the afterlife, but
Confucianism deals more with life on earth.

In 440 BC Taoism became a state religion, at which time
people venerated Lao-tze as a deity.

The central principle of Taoism teaches that all life relates
to an inseparable whole, an interconnected unity that has its
source in a deep, mysterious, and essentially inexplicable reality,
which is the Tao itself. This principle encompasses everything
conceivable. Westerners often best understand this in terms of
God, Universal Mind, or Absolute Reality. Hindus might make

the comparison to Brahman. Taoism teaches that the universe operates within a set of immutable natural laws. Mankind can gain knowledge of these laws and align themselves with the principles and live in harmony with the Tao. Thus man's way becomes *The Way*, a full expression of the Tao.

In Taoism everything constantly changes. Absolute stillness doesn't exist. All things, including the universe, change all the time. Relative stability becomes possible by reaching harmony between Yin and Yang, which Taoists believe are opposite but related natural forces in the universe.

Western and Chinese philosophies differ in a critical way. The West treats individuals as independent and separate entities. Chinese treat individuals as an interrelated element of the whole universe. While Western philosophy centres on self, thus placing blame on others, Chinese tend to merge self with society so that self diminishes or disappears.

Taoism is the basis for traditional Chinese medicine and Tai Chi. Traditional Chinese medicine teaches that illness arises from blockages or lack of balance in the body's *chi* or intrinsic energy. Tai Chi is an exercise system that proponents believe balances the energy flow.

 This historic symbol of Taoism, in fact, preceded Taoism by two thousand years. Yin, the dark side, symbolizes the breath that formed the earth, while Yang, the light side, represents the breath that formed the heavens. They symbolize pairs of opposites that occur throughout the universe: good and evil, light and dark, male and female. Intervention by humans upsets the balances of Yin and Yang. The symbol of Taoism represents Yin and Yang in balance.

Buddhism

Buddhism began in India about 500 BC by the Buddha who taught a continuous cycle of death and rebirth. He believed that each person's behaviour and position in previous lives determined his or her position and well-being in the present life. A good life might lead to rebirth as a wise and wealthy person, while a bad life might lead to rebirth as a poor and sickly person. Buddha also believed that pain and suffering are parts of a person's life—one could only escape human suffering by giving up worldly desires such as power, wealth, and beauty. This way, one could achieve perfect peace and happiness.

Buddhism first entered China about AD 65. Emperor Ming of the Han Dynasty invited two Indian monks to establish a monastery. Initially Buddhism had little influence in China. With the downfall of the Han Dynasty in AD 220 Buddhism spread throughout China. By the late fourth century, Buddhism had become very popular, especially in the northwest region of China. From there it spread to Japan and Korea.

Edicts against foreign religions by various emperors eventually almost completely eliminated Buddhism from China.

Ancestor worship
Ancestor worship has characterized Chinese culture since the earliest of times, either coexisting with other religions or philosophies, or merging with them. In its simplest form it honours the family and reverences the wisdom of the elders. In its more complex form it takes on the trappings of a religious system, but is generally practiced within the family. Before eating, family members will place plates of food before pictures of their ancestors, showing a willingness to provide for the ancestors in their afterlife. Once or twice a year, families visit grave sites and conduct elaborate rituals, presenting food and other things that they feel the ancestors will need. They kowtow—kneeling and touching their heads to the ground—to express worship or submission.

The worshippers participate as a filial duty, but typically without any sense of fear or desire for gain. However, some will burn incense daily and pray to their ancestors for help and guidance.

PART 2: MAKING READY

The gem cannot be polished without friction, nor man
perfected without trials.
—Confucius

Lord, we know what we are, but know not what we may be.
—Shakespeare

Train a child in the way he should go, and
when he is old he will not turn from it.
—Proverbs 22:6

CHAPTER 4 : *A Boy and His Roots*

*Alexander Pope said, "Just as the twig is bent,
the tree's inclined."*

On October 29, 1932, the baby's cry broke the tension in the room. The midwife, holding the tiny body in her arms, said, "He lives!" but the child's wail overwhelmed her words.

"Praise God," whispered the mother, relaxing now the hard work of giving birth had ended. The discomfort remained, but the joy of a new life soon began pushing into memory the pangs of pain that had thrust Baby Bao-wha into the world. Mother and Father Chang glowed with the sincere pride of the humble.

***

Teng-xian, Shandong, China
Human lives, like the seeds in the parable, fall on many kinds of soil. Bao-wha, in God's plan, had fallen on the fertile ground of the Province of Shandong[24]; for him life began within the sheltering walls of a seminary; unlike most Chinese babies born that day, he became part of the third generation of a Christian family—yet remained part of a rich culture with roots extending five millennia into the mists of time. He would grow tall, like his ancestors from northern China, and experience the turmoil that has characterized his land and especially his province.

Shandong Province has many geographical, social, and historical claims to fame. Located on the vast expanse of the North China Plain, Shandong juts almost as far into the Yellow Sea as it reaches inland—the peninsula, shaped like the head of a turtle, points toward Korea, as though wanting to swim away from the rest of China. The alluvial flood plain of the Yellow River dominates the area. That great river has brought both bounty and destruction to the land and its people.

Completely fickle, it has changed its route 26 times in its history, and six times its mouth has shifted from one side of the peninsula to the other, from North Shandong to South

Shandong. At the river's whim, it brings fertile soil or devastating floods.

The climate appears equally as erratic, providing hot and humid summers followed by cold and dry winters, but with an annual rainfall that exhibits extreme variations. In 1876 the lack of rain resulted in the death of nearly two million people. In 1898 a scorching drought gripped the area, followed in 1899 by a flood of the entire Shandong plain.

The earliest of China's recorded civilizations appeared along the banks of the Yellow River. Historically and currently among China's most populous provinces, it has always had great influence on the rest of the country. Confucius was born there. Foreign powers established themselves on its coastlines and missionary forces paid it special attention in the latter 1800s and early 1900s. The Boxer rebellion arose there, partly in response to the incursion of foreigners.

All this became Bao-wha's physical, historical, and cultural heritage.

The missionaries came
Without the powerful influence of living representatives of the risen Christ, Bao-wha might have arrived, grown up, lived, and died without leaving his corner of Shandong. Christ walked the byways of Shandong through the lives of American Presbyterian missionaries.

Female missionaries typically outnumber their male opposites. Hindered in most cultures from evangelizing men, women evangelize women as a bridge to their target group. Cultural constraints mean that the men among the missionary force most often approach the elite of the society—the opinion leaders, the chiefs—while women focus on the poor or downtrodden. Grace Mary Rowley from California, a missionary with the Presbyterian Church of the USA, and a graduate of Occidental University, followed that pattern when in 1910 she arrived in Weisien—a remote village in Shandong province. Her first convert in that village was a woman from a poor family. Five years later she won the woman's husband. When a son of the family—Chang Hsueh Kung, born the year of the great Shandong flood—began to show promise, she helped fund his education, first at Shandong Christian University in Tsinan, then eventually sponsored him to study at Princeton Theological Seminary in the United States.

Grace Rowley had effectively crossed the cultural bridge and won for Christ a family that would become prominent in Chinese Christian circles.

Another American Presbyterian missionary, Dr. W.M. Hayes, also contributed to the Christian life of the Chang family. He saw the need of a seminary to train Chinese high-school and college graduates for ministry. With a group of like-minded fellow workers, he established the Northern China Theological Seminary to provide sound theological education committed to the authority of Scripture and to the *Westminster Confession of Faith*.

The Presbyterians, and indeed all other missionary organizations, had experienced a great recovery following the Boxer rebellion. By 1920, the Presbyterian Church of the USA had 579 missionaries in China—more than half of the total mission personnel stationed in China from all branches of Presbyterian churches worldwide. In Shandong alone they had a force of 136 workers, by far the largest number among all mission organizations working in that province.

Chang Hsueh Kung had married Liang Hui Ting. By 1928 they had produced five children, three boys and two girls. That year Chang made a momentous decision—encouraged by Grace Rowley and the promise of financial support, he would leave his wife and family in China and journey to the United States to study at Princeton Theological Seminary.

During his time at Princeton, a debate raged over mod-ernism in the Presbyterian denomination—a controversy that also influenced the seminary. In 1929 a group of conservative faculty members, under the leadership of J. Gresham Machen, left Princeton and founded the Westminster Theological Seminary in Philadelphia. Chang, concerned that the theology of the day had limited his understanding of evangelical principles, completed his work at Princeton and then studied for a few months at Moody Bible Institute in Chicago before returning to China. While there he wrote a book on personal evangelism.

Back in China, Professor Chang published his book, settled in as vice-principal of Northern China Theological Seminary, and added Bao-wha to his family. But for a man born during Shandong's great flood and the Boxer rebellion—and in a province that had proven pivotal to Chinese history—the settled life would not last.

All this provided the spiritual and family heritage that nurtured Bao-wha.

The good years
At age five, Bao-wha knew nothing of the political turmoil that raged in China: the horror of the Long March; the constant skirmishes between the private armies of warlords; and the clashes between Nationalist and Communist forces. Neither had he knowledge of the Japanese in Manchuria poised to strike into China proper. But he did understand the joy, the music, and the laughter that rebounded from the walls of the Chang home.

He pushed his tiny body against the piano stool to get closer to his sister, Bao-yin,[25] and threw back his head, adding his soprano voice to the harmonious mix. His older brothers struggled to reach the bass notes, his mother and sisters blended in their soprano and alto voices creating a sound that would challenge an angel choir—at least Bao-wha thought so.

The great hymn ended in a mighty amen and the room became silent, almost as if the performance had awed the participants themselves. Bao-yin's hand fell on Bao-wha's shoulder. She smiled down on him and said, "Little brother, you did a great job. I think it's time for you to join our family group when we perform in churches."

Realizing that she might have spoken out of turn, that she might have usurped her father's authority, she glanced toward him, but the sparkle in his eyes assured her she had made a right choice.

"Let's gather for the family devotions—we can practice

again later," Father said.

As Bao-yin sat next to her mother, her father leaned across to her and said, "Daughter, feel free to make the musical decisions. You're the one who studied music with Missionary Watson, so I think of you as the family expert."

As the weeks and months slipped by, Bao-wha became an integral part of the family singing team, often taking solo parts. Even today he remembers as highlights of his life the times singing about the piano and the daily family devotions with his father's Bible stories and even more singing. In a thoughtful moment, his mind slips back over the years and he says, "I really appreciate that God put me in that family."

Life drifted along with the same innocence and sense of wonder and adventure experienced by children the world over. During bright spring days Bao-wha joined with his friends in raiding birds' nests, each one testing his nerve to see who could climb highest and collect the greatest number of eggs. In the heat of summer when the fledglings had left nests that the parent birds had hidden from the eyes of the human fledglings, the boys turned their interests to catching grasshoppers. In the fall, football vied for attention with the opening of school. Without money to buy the real thing, they begged heavy pieces of cloth from their mothers and sewed them into footballs. The little pocket money they had came from papers collected and sold at the paper mill. As the footballs began to disintegrate and the cutting edge of winter's cold arrived pushing the average temperature below zero degrees Celsius, the young adventurers turned their attention to school and other indoor activities.

Bao-wha attended the primary school led by seminary students within the mission compound. The students taught as a contribution toward their seminary costs. Their emphasis and application of Christianity to daily living further augmented the biblical teaching received at home. But Bao-wha learned best from his greatest hero, his father.

Throughout the year, the senior Chang made regular preaching trips into the countryside, often taking family members with him. When Bao-wha had barely begun primary school, his father asked him to go along to teach the children while he preached to the adults. Bao-wha invited a young friend, Hung Dai-wei,[26] to go with him. Dai-wei, the son of a custodian who worked at the seminary, took the challenge and joined the team. They walked for about two hours before reaching the village. While Bao-wha's father concerned himself with the adults, the two youngsters taught the children to sing Christian songs and told them Bible stories.

The young Bao-wha had begun his career as an evangelist. But those trips also brought him face-to-face with the sordid side of life in China—with destitution and death.

Lessons learned

Bao-wha strained to maintain the pace set by Hsueh Kung. Two of his steps barely matched each giant stride of his father. *I need a bicycle, a car, or even a locomotive*, he thought. *Yeah, a locomotive.* He loved to sit by the railway track outside the seminary wall and watch the great engines thundering past. He began to feel like a steam engine, each breath bursting from him like spent steam, and each thrust of a leg and foot against the ground like a mighty cylinder and connecting rod—well, maybe like a miniature cylinder and connecting rod.

Wanting to let loose a great blast on his imaginary engine whistle, he opened his mouth but only three limp words came out, "Father, wait up!"

Hsueh Kung stopped instantly and turned to the struggling youngster. "My goodness son, you are puffing away like a . . . like a . . ."

"Like a steam engine," the boy responded.

"Bless you son, we'll slow down just a little. If we're late the people will wait for us."

Hand in hand the two continued on, but they didn't get far. A woman and four boys stood at the roadside begging, their hands outstretched. Beside them on the ground lay the body of a man, stiff and straight with hands folded.

Bao-wha felt his father's hand tighten on his. A tickling sensation ran up his spine. He asked, "Father, does he sleep?"

but somehow he knew better.

"He is dead, Son."

"Why don't they take him to the cemetery and bury him?"

"Because they have no money and no family to help them. They hope a passerby will take pity on them."

"We must hurry on Father. We'll be late."

"No, we must stay and help. God has placed them in our way."

Hsueh Kung spoke briefly with the woman and her sons, then said simply, "Come follow me."

Bao-wha felt another chill run up his spine, but this time not because of fear. "*My father*, he thought, *spoke with such love and authority—he sounded almost like Jesus speaking.*"

Hsueh Kung took them to the nearby village and helped bury the dead husband and father. After visiting the hovel that had been their home to gather their pitiful belongings, he took them back to the seminary.

"Where will they live?" Bao-wha asked on the return journey.

"We will find something. God will provide a place for them."

"Father, why did you . . . why did we help them?" Bao-wha said, feeling a need to identify with his father in the strange happenings of this afternoon.

"Jesus told us to. He said, 'Whatever you do for the least of these, you do for me.' When we help them, it is as though we had met Jesus along the way and helped him. Serving others is really an act of worship."

During the long walk home, Bao-wha said little, for his young mind struggled with the profound concepts of service and worship. As the small procession of father and son and mother and four sons turned to enter the seminary gate, they passed the mill. Bao-wha pulled on his father's hand to stop him. "Then this mill is like a church."

"What do you mean son?"

"You had it built to help the farmers—to give them a place to grind their grain. So isn't that an act of worship?"

Hsueh Kung squeezed his son's hand. "Yes son. Every time

the great millstone turns, it praises God."

For Bao-wha, lessons in the holistic gospel had only just begun. In the days that followed, his father oversaw construction of a small cottage in the corner of their garden for the Chan family, the grieving mother and her sons. They soon became a vital part of Bao-wha's life for Mrs. Chan became nanny to Bao-wha and his siblings. The oldest Chan boy, named by his mother "Chan Number Three" because her first two sons had died, became the Chang family cook. He also helped take care of Bao-wha and the other children and did so with the strong personality of a disciplinarian.

One bright fall day, Bao-wha raced past his house in pursuit of Dai-wei who had grabbed the bedraggled football and yelled, "Can't catch me!"

The two sped through the gate into Mother's vegetable garden. With careless abandon they raced between rows of cabbages and bok choy—they had entered forbidden territory.

"Bao-wha, Dai-wei, stop!"

The two intruders slid to a halt and looked about for the source of the command. They saw Chan Number Three striding purposefully from the house, carrying a large wooden spoon and wearing an apron. He approached until he stood before them, brandishing the spoon. Bao-wha felt an odd prickling sensation in his backside as he watched the potential weapon.

Number Three spoke, "You boys know you must not play in the garden. It's a good thing I saw you from the kitchen window before you did any damage. All of us, and many other people, depend on this garden to supply food during the winter."

The boys said nothing. They just stared at the ground, although Bao-wha stole a peek at the wooden spoon.

Number Three continued, "Not only that, but you're standing right in the middle of the Lord's cabbages."

Dai-wei, still gripping the football, looked up and said, "The Lord's cabbages?"

Bao-wha bit his lip. He wanted to warn Dai-wei not to talk back to the cook.

"Yes the Lord's cabbages," said Number Three. "Do you

see these ten rows of cabbages?"

Bao-wha's eyes followed ten long rows, reaching right back to the Chan's little house at the foot of the garden.

"The two rows you are standing between belong to the Lord. Tomorrow Mrs. Chang and I will harvest them and take them to the church to be given to needy people. She always gives the garden's first produce to the Lord. She practices tithing."

Number Three waved the wooden spoon to dismiss the boys. Chastised, they slipped from the garden, but Dai-wei wrinkled his brow in puzzlement. He'd done some basic arithmetic.

Out of sight of the garden the boys stopped. Dai-Wei spoke, "A tithe means one-tenth. If your mother gives two rows out of ten, wouldn't that be two-tenths?"

Bao-wha grabbed the football from Dai-wei, "Mother and Father always do more than God expects of them," he said, taking off at a run toward the seminary main gate.

Disaster

Even while the Chang family enjoyed those good years, China had begun to move into another cycle of terror. In 1937, the Japanese invaded China proper from their bases in Manchuria. It didn't take them long to occupy the major coastal cities and begin to commit terrible atrocities. In December of that year they took Nanjing. A massacre that lasted for six weeks and claimed hundreds of thousands of lives.[27]

The Japanese then pressed north into Shandong but met strong Chinese resistance. Although the invaders eventually overcame, it granted the residents of Teng-xian an extended time of peace. When the Japanese finally arrived, they brought about great changes in life at the seminary.

Japan, not wishing to provoke the United States into entering the war, respected the seminary as American property. Even before the invaders approached, the missionaries who lived within the compound had made sure the US flag flew at the main gate. Now viewed as American territory, the seminary became a safe haven for many Chinese who feared the Japanese army. As refugees arrived, Chang Hsueh Kung gave them shelter until nearly three thousand filled every spare corner of the mission compound. Professor Chang even turned his house over to the refugees and, with his family, moved into the second storey of the seminary dormitory.

Frustrated by Chang's non-cooperation and hoping to further terrify the residents of the seminary compound, the Japanese commander marched hundreds of Chinese people along the railway track adjacent to the compound, machine-gunned them, and burned the bodies. Bao-wha from his hiding place in the attic became another witness to the horror of war, to man's inhumanity to man.

From the wok into the fire

Encouraged by their victories in China and Southeast Asia, Japan provoked the Americans into the war by attacking Pearl Harbour in December of 1941[28]. This changed everything at the seminary. The missionaries appointed Chang Hsueh Kung Principal of the seminary and most of them left the country. Those who dared to remain soon found themselves in Japanese internment camps. The refugees scattered. The total responsibility for the missionary compound, the seminary, and all associated ministries now fell on Professor Chang. He had to find the finances to keep things going, and he had little in the way of assets—essentially just his faith.

He would need to call on all that faith for the immediate challenge—the Japanese commander had demanded an interview.

Professor Chang waited for the Japanese officer. Although outwardly calm, fear gripped him internally. He felt little concern for his life—he expected the Japanese to shoot him for the way he had defied them. Then his whole body shuddered; getting shot might be the easy way out. He had heard stories of Japanese soldiers torturing pastors, men he knew, by forcing water and ground chili peppers into their noses and throats until it bloated their stomachs. To increase the pain, the tormentors then pounded on the suffering men's stomachs.

Chang's body reacted to his mental anguish by shooting

sympathetic pains through his nose, throat, and stomach. He shook it off, but distress for his family soon took over, and he silently prayed for them. Then his thoughts moved to his friends, the workers at the seminary, the orphans in the girls' home, and the lepers in the leper colony.

The commander entered the room and stood before Professor Chang. Following ancient Asian custom, they each bowed as though meeting an old friend rather than a sworn enemy. Chang had heard stories of westerners in similar circumstances who had refused to bow and met with dire consequences, but he saw it as culturally correct and a Christian duty to show respect, even to an enemy.

The commander spoke through an interpreter. "The army of His Imperial Majesty has need of space, so I am appropriating your compound. I order you to evacuate it."

The professor responded with dignity, "We will begin immediately to vacate the compound."

The commander continued, "I also order you to dig a trench so we can shoot and bury all the inmates of the leper colony."

Chang shuddered, a picture of the earlier massacre flashed across his mind. He thought quickly, "If you will permit me to make a suggestion that will cause you less trouble, I will seal off the leper compound except for one door and will provide for those within. You can post a guard who can shoot anyone who leaves by that door."

To his great relief, the commander agreed, but had one more condition. "You also have an orphanage, I would like to inspect that so I can determine its disposition."

"I will make those arrangements," Chang replied.

He left the interview with mixed feelings. He was alive. He had saved the lepers, but he feared for the young women in the orphanage. He suspected the commander wanted them as "comfort women" to live in so-called army comfort stations—in reality, military brothels. The professor would need to move very quickly.

He first set in motion the evacuation of the compound, then secretly removed the older girls from the orphanage and hid them. As an additional safety factor he adopted them. When the Japanese authorities later visited the orphanage, they showed no interest in the younger girls still living there. Professor Chang had guessed correctly.

The Japanese removed the high-quality pews from the church, shipped them to Japan, and turned the church into a stable.

Not only did Chang Hsueh Kung manage to protect the orphanage and the leper colony, he relocated the seminary to the Women's Learning Centre and continued operating it throughout the duration of the war.

New Movements

Across China the war with Japan disrupted the missionary program. While many foreign missionaries returned home, many others spent the duration of the war in Japanese concentration camps. A few, depending on their location, continued ministering, but with severe restrictions. For the most part, Chinese Christians, like Chang Hsueh Kung, knew they had to find other means of support if they wanted to keep their ministries alive and propagating. Across the land, indigenous groups began emerging, like those of the Little Flock of Ni To-sheng (Watchman Nee), Jesus Family, Wang Ming Dao's local churches, and the Chinese Native Evangelistic Crusade (CNEC).

Duncan McRoberts, a missionary who remained in China, witnessed the fruitful ministry of the Chinese pastors bringing other Chinese to the Lord. He then caught the vision: he saw the strength of one native sharing the good news with another native. He also discovered a British engineer, Fred Savage, who gave one-third of his salary to support Chinese evangelists while he was working in Shanghai. McRoberts reported Fred Savage's one-man effort to members of the Christian Business Men's Committee (CBMC) in Seattle, North America. These men had earlier on formed a prayer group to pray for the lost souls in China. Led by

Dr. N.A. Jepson, they prayed and realized it was God's purpose to launch a missionary endeavour to assist the Chinese nationals to work among their own people.[29]

They began by supporting two Chinese pastors: the Reverend Calvin Chao who later led the Student Union and the Reverend Chang Hsueh Kung. With assistance from CNEC, Professor Chang maintained some of the ministries associated with the Northern China Theological Seminary despite the Japanese occupation of the major facilities.

The Japanese occupation would not last. The Western world and China would win the war against Japan, but would it bring a better life for the Chinese people? And what about the Christians among them?

CHAPTER 5 : *Fleeing*

Psalm 23:4 says, "Even though I walk through the valley of the shadow of death, I will fear no evil, for you are with me."

During the war with Japan, Communist and Nationalist forces had ceased fighting each other and turned their attention to the Japanese. However, during that time the Communists consolidated their hold on the north. Following victory against Japan, they resumed the civil war against the Nationalists and pressed southward. On Christmas Eve of 1945 they arrived in Teng-xian.

Time to move on

Chang Hsueh Kung had no illusions about the Communists. He would remain and hold together the remnants of the ministry, but he realized such a decision would endanger the oldest of those who still remained at home—Bao-wha and Bao-an. Would the Communist forces press them into military service? Would he lose them in a senseless civil war? Drastic circumstances demanded drastic action. Two sons must immediately flee south to join Bao-yin who taught in a music school in Nanjing, at that time the capital for the Nationalists under Chiang Kai-shek.

Bao-wha and his older brother Bao-an stood in the front hallway facing their father. Both carried satchels containing changes of clothes, blankets, and food. Chang spoke to the older boy, "Bao-An, you are of military age. The Communists won't hesitate to train you as a soldier and put you into action fighting your own countrymen, so use extreme care should you encounter communist patrols. And take good care of your brother."

Chang turned his attention to the younger boy, "Even you, Bao-wha, at age thirteen stand in danger of a similar plight. Think of yourself as a soldier of Jesus Christ making your way through enemy territory."

Bao-wha's mother held him tightly. She wept as she thought of him as a refugee travelling three hundred kilometres in winter, seeking food and shelter wherever he could find it. "Remember," she said, rubbing her left hand over his trousers against his thigh. "It's right here beneath the lining."

Bao-wha's eyes followed her fingers. He could not help but notice her ring finger, now without the wedding band.

His mother continued speaking, "I have sewn my gold wedding ring into the lining of your trousers. If you need money for food, sell it."

Professor Chang, understanding this display of mother love and sacrifice, said, "We're putting the boys in God's care, Mother. After all, we have many friends between here and Nanjing who will take the boys in and feed them."

Bao-wha hugged his mother. In a moment he would step out the door into a great adventure.

It didn't take long before the adventure began turning sour and he started wishing himself back home. The cold cut through his jacket. His feet ached. Hunger tugged at his stomach. Even the moon looked cold and lonely as it stared down on the snow-covered countryside. The boys trudged onward, straight toward a roadblock of battle-hardened and trigger-happy fighting men.

The soldiers blocked their way. The hunger in Bao-wha's stomach turned to fear and his mouth refused to open, but Bao-an exercised his authority as leader and spoke. "We're students going home for the holidays. We have to walk, for we have no money for trains. We're not armed; see, all we have are a few clothes."

The boys held out their satchels. While holding them at gunpoint, the soldiers deliberated their fate, but soon decided the two youths presented no threat and waved them on.

Relief flooded through the young refugees as they continued down the road. In better times they had travelled this same route as companions to their father on preaching tours. The cold and hunger returned, but they knew people in the village ahead—there they would find refuge for the night.

It took days to reach Nanjing. They received shelter and encouragement in the homes of Christians who knew their father. They encountered many folk along the way who had found refuge in the seminary during the Japanese occupation, people who willingly returned the kindness to Professor Chang's sons.

Most of the time the boys walked, often pushing a hand cart with the aid of people who recognized them and insisted on accompanying them part way. Occasionally they hitched rides on farm carts; too often they heard gunfire and felt fear. The worst moment occurred as they crossed a lake in a borrowed rowboat. When gunfire erupted on the shore, thinking a Communist patrol had spotted them, they rowed frantically for the opposite side.

After about ten days, dirty and tired, and feeling like hunted animals, they reached the banks of the Yangtze River and crossed from disputed land to Nationalist territory in a steamer loaded with other fleeing refugees.

Safely in Nanjing with Bao-yin, and with the bulk of the Communist army far to the north, they felt safe and made plans for the future. Bao-wha began a new life by entering junior high and moving into a dormitory.

Back in Teng-xian life became increasingly difficult for the remaining members of the Chang family. The parents watched with grave misgiving the manipulation of the family and society by the victorious Communist rulers. During the next few months they managed to evacuate the younger children to Nanjing and withdraw from ministry responsibilities. When they could no longer contribute, they too fled to the south, reuniting the family in Nanjing less than one year after Bao-wha's arrival.

Despite the civil war raging to the north, life became very exciting for the Chang family. Their arrival coincided with a revival that was spreading through the university community. The newly-formed Chinese Inter-Varsity Fellowship under the leadership of Rev. Calvin Chao had struck a chord with students tired of war and searching for better answers. China had never seen anything like it—and never had Bao-wha! He responded to the gospel and grew under the teaching and fervour of the young Christians around him.

Things moved very quickly. Chang Hsueh Kung accepted the leadership of a large Nanjing church and began ministering to great numbers of youthful new converts. Many of these young people wanted more training. Fred Savage and other leaders of the China Native Evangelistic Crusade turned to Chang: "Will you become the principal of a new seminary to train these students?"

Chang needed no persuasion. They rented an old hotel and began the Tai-tung Theological Seminary with 50 students.

The Crusade had 13 evangelistic teams or "bands" that travelled to the interior provinces of China. They reported conversions in places that had no established Christian ministries. Students of the Tai-Tung Seminary formed similar groups and went far afield during the school holidays, using their trumpets and accordions to attract crowds in the villages.

In addition to his seminary work, Professor Chang continued his ministry in the Nanjing church. As the crowds grew, the church made plans to build a large central church. Each month Chang ministered to high-level Nationalist leaders, including Chiang Kai-shek.[30]

Throughout the next two years, the Communist armies pressed southward, taking city after city and pressing relentlessly toward the Yangtze River that flows from west to east, dividing northern China from the south. In Nanjing tensions grew. The Nationalist government, always unstable at best and riddled with corruption, began losing what little control it had. In a state of bankruptcy, the government simply began printing more money. The resulting hyper inflation crippled trade—rice became scarce.

In the seminary and churches, around the dinner tables, and wherever Christians met, people talked of potential problems under communism. Some argued. "This is a different breed of communism, not at all like the Russian kind that hates Christianity and tries to exterminate it."

Another countered, "That might be, but they probably won't permit Bible schools and seminaries."

Even more pessimistically someone added, "They might go much further than that and close all the churches. If we stay, we'll have to meet secretly."

On the backs of the peasants and common people

It didn't seem to matter who ruled China, the common people always carried the greatest burdens. Note what one writer says:

In the cities labourers were treated little better than beasts of burden; children were used as slave labour in factories, standing at machines for 12 or 13 hours a day and sleeping under them at night; women and children were sold as concubines, prostitutes or domestic slaves; the destitute and starving died on the streets of Chinese cities and strikes were ruthlessly suppressed by foreign and Chinese factory owners.

In the countryside the . . . 'government' . . . ruled in collusion with the landlords and moneylenders and their private armed guards. Attempts at reform were blocked because it was not in their interest to reduce rents or allow the establishment of rural banks with low interest rates for peasants. . . . Peasant revolts were often dealt with by the private armies and gangs retained by many landlords, while the peasants' wives and children were taken into the land-lords' households as domestic slaves in lieu of debts.*

This description does not deal with the China under the Manchu Dynasty, the occupying Japanese, or the communists. It describes conditions under a leader generally highly respected among western nations—Chiang Kai-shek.

But should we place the blame solely on Chiang? Fighting Communists and Japanese kept him so occupied much of the governing fell to local warlords who gave him only superficial allegiance.

* pages 22, 23, Samagalski et al—China, a Travel Survival Kit.

Those who depended on financial assistance commented. "If the communists take over, and it looks like they will, we'll be in real danger if we have anything to do with western missionaries. Even taking money from outside sources will be impossible."

A few tried to look on the bright side. "But they are Chinese even though they are communists, surely things will never again get as bad as they were under the Japanese Imperial Army."

Even as people debated, refugees poured across the river into Nanjing. They told horror stories of destruction of family life under the Communists, persecution of Christians, expropriation of private property, forced communal living, and imprisonment or re-education of those who dissented.

Although Professor Chang joined the discussions, internally he already knew the answers. He had tried to continue his ministry under communism in Teng-xian without success. Should they cross the river, he would once again move southward, taking with him not just his family, but the student body. He hoped Chiang Kai-shek might yet regroup his forces and drive the Communists back. But if that failed and the Communists eventually overran all of China, he needed more time to train his students, to equip them for whatever lay ahead.

Within two years of the Changs' arrival in Nanjing the communist forces began crossing the Yangtze. The Nationalist army withdrew in disarray, and the Chang family again joined the southern flood of refugees. The family and 70 students who had elected to travel to Changsha, a distance of nearly eight hundred kilometres, planned to meet at the Bible school operated by the Bible Institute of Los Angeles.[31] The group split up and scrambled for room on trains, making it out of town just before the Communists shut down all the rail lines to the south.

Bao-wha travelled overnight on a train, tied to the outside with a rope, afraid to sleep for fear of falling off. In comparison, his mother found passage in more comfortable circumstances— inside a box car. Confusion reigned. Families and friends became separated. Many left desperate messages scribbled on the pillars and walls of the railway stations. All the Chang family members and the students travelling with them arrived safely, although they had many frightening stories to tell.

While in Changsha they lived in the Hunan Bible School, which graciously shared its facilities with the seminary. Bao-wha did not attend school during the nine months they stayed there. In June of 1949 the advancing Communists precipitated another move.

And again

It gets worse every time we do this. One day we will have to stop running, thought Professor Chang as he surveyed the Changsha railway station. People carrying suitcases, boxes tied with ropes, bags, and small, crying children milled about. He felt heavy and tired, *It's not just that I'm getting older,* he thought. *It's all the extra things I'm carrying in my pockets and sewn into my clothes.* He smiled as he thought of his resourceful wife, Liang Hui Ting, sewing her life's savings of silver dollars into the clothes of each family member.

Chang continued his survey of potential transportation by pushing through the crowd toward the platform. Armed officials of the fleeing Nationalist government guarded the train, waving back the frantic mob. "This train is for government officials and their families only. Wait for the next train."

If there ever is another train, Chang thought. *We must move quickly, or we will never get out of here.*

Chang regrouped his dwindling student body, staff, and family members for the last time in Changsha. "We will meet at the Christian and Missionary Alliance Bible School in Guilin. Travel in small groups using whatever method you can find. If you walk, avoid the main roads. You are on your own until we reunite in Guilin."

Professor Chang spread his arms as if to embrace the whole group and prayed for their safety. Within minutes they had gathered their scant belongings, assembled into assigned groups, and melded into the fleeing throng. Chang had selected six of the keenest students as travel companions. He would take advantage of every minute to teach them along the way. They

Another family on the move

Right across China many families fled for various reasons from the Japanese and communist advances—that included the parents and sisters of Liu Nien-chang, born in Shanghai in 1934. No one could have guessed that the paths of Chang Bao-wha and Liu Nien-chang would one day cross. The Liu's had moved from Nanjing so Nien-chang's father, Liu Yu-wan, could take a position with the Institute of Pacific relations. He had studied at Bejing University and in the United States. Her mother, Lee Chee-mung, attended normal school and became a teacher. Mr. Liu, uncomfortable when the Institute of Pacific relations began to show leftist leanings, looked elsewhere.

The Japanese invasion caught Liu in Chongqing* and his wife and family of four girls in Kowloon across from the island of Hong Kong. When the Japanese came to the Kowloon flat and ordered them to vacate it, they temporarily moved in with another family who had a larger place. Lee Chee-mung, seeing no future remaining under the Japanese, took three of her daughters, joined a group of bank employees, and began walking to Chongqing—a distance of over eight hundred kilometres.

When the children could walk no further, their mother hired peasant women to carry them in sedan chairs. They travelled part way by truck and train and then along the Yangtze River by boat. During much of the trip, the girls remained hidden to avoid detection by the Japanese soldiers. They rented a house in Chongqing and, while there, Mother home-schooled the children.

When the war with Japan ended, the family returned to Nanjing. Soon Mr. Liu joined the foreign service, accepted a post in Korea, and moved there with his family, where they stayed for four years. Next, he took a post at the United Nations, moving to the United States with his family. Years later, Nien-chang and Bao-wha met in California.

* Formerly spelled *Chungking*.

managed to board a train, but they soon found themselves side-tracked and shunted into a railway yard, while the escaping government and military personnel rushed by on the main line. For one week they immersed themselves in studies, leaving the train only to take toilet breaks and scavenge for food.

***

For Bao-wha fleeing ahead of the advancing Communist forces had become routine; he faced it with typical teenage bravado. But this ride would tax him as none other. Refugees thronged the railway platform, fighting for space on the train. People swarmed aboard like insects on an anthill. They filled every available space—on the carriage roofs, on the couplings between the coaches. Others "rode the rods" by placing boards on chassis members beneath the carriages and lying in the restricted space.

Bao-wha wondered about other family members as he shouldered through the crowds, working his way closer to the train in hope of boarding. He spied a free space between the tender and the engine and made for it. As soot from the engine's stack began covering him, he wondered about his choice position. He didn't wonder long. The engine driver called over the din of the crowd and the escaping steam, "Kid, if you expect to stay there, you'll have to pay me for it."

Bao-wha fumbled for money from his limited supply and extracted enough to meet the engineer's demands. The whistle blew, steam hissed into the big cylinders, and the engine moved ahead, taking up slack from the couplings. The train began its journey.

At the next major stop the crew changed. A new engineer walked about the engine before mounting the cab and stopped near Bao-wha still clinging to his precarious perch.

"I need money if you expect to ride there," he said.

"I paid the last driver! He took my money."

The engine driver scowled, "I'm in charge now. If you want to ride, pay me or get off."

Bao-wha couldn't afford to pay more and dropped to the

ground. Panic gripped him as he elbowed his way back through the mob along the platform. Each carriage bulged with human bodies. Mothers called out to lost children, people scrambled to collect personal belongings that had fallen from broken cases, the old and injured teetered on canes and crutches. Confusion, distress, and anguish dominated. Bao-wha, responding to years of his father's training, wanted to help, but what could he do?

He refocused on his own plight when the whistle shrieked and the coaches began to tremble as the engine strained against the great load. In a moment the train began moving forward, and people stepped back in despair. Suddenly someone caught his arm and propelled him toward the moving train.

A voice yelled in his ear, "Grab the stair rail as it goes by, Bao-wha. We'll jump onto the outside step."

Relief flooded through Bao-wha. Wong, a seminary student, had spotted him and rushed to his rescue. Together they clung to the stair rails as the train gathered speed. The wind tore at their thin raincoats, cinders stung their faces, their bodies passed within a hand span of coaches parked on sidings, and the steps shook with the irregularities of the tracks. But they had made their choice and they hung on—their lives counted on it. And this might well be the last train to pass this station for Guilin.

Wong yelled to Bao-wha over the rattle of the wheels, "I have some rope in my bag. When we get to the next stop, we can tie ourselves to the steps for the night."

For days Bao-wha and Wong clung to the refugee train. Cold at night, often soaked by rain, coated with soot and dirt, discouraged and hungry, they soldiered on. At night when the train moved, one remained awake to watch the other who rested fitfully, head against the coach, body straining against the ropes that bound him to the train steps. Each time the sleeper began to slip, the watcher pinched him to wake him. Although Guilin lay approximately four hundred kilometres from Changsha, the train travelled much further, avoiding blocked tracks and searching out a safer route.

The train stopped often: at times to wait on a siding to allow a military train the right-of-way; often while the engineer tried to determine the state of the line ahead; frequently while he negotiated for coal and water from those who controlled the dwindling supply; and often while he demanded additional money from the passengers.

One morning the youthful travellers heard a terrible wailing coming from under their coach. When the train stopped to refuel and take on water for the boiler and the passengers scrambled off for drinking water and to relieve themselves, they learned of the tragedy. A woman, overcome by sleep, had dropped her baby to its death beneath the wheels. On at least one occasion, several people riding on top of the coach died as the train sped through a low tunnel. Death rode as an unwanted passenger on every refugee train.

Despite the suffering and death all around them, the boys worked hard to maintain their spirits. They sang hymns, quoted Scripture, and praised God that he had brought them safely thus far. When the weather cleared and a bright sun illuminated the beautiful Chinese countryside, Bao-wha, remembered and quoted the words of the Psalm, "I lift up my eyes to the hills— where does my help come from? My help comes from the Lord, the maker of heaven and earth."

He felt God's presence and knew his parents would not cease praying for him.

The final night of the trip seemed like a nightmare to Bao-wha. With rain pelting down the weary twosome huddled at a roadside trying for a few hours sleep. Refugees continued to press southward, terrified the conquering Communist armies would overtake them. The boys had neither food nor money— not that money would help much, prices had made even a handful of rice beyond the reach of most people. In any case, had they either food or money, army deserters would have taken it from them. Families had become separated, pandemonium ruled; society seemed to have only one dictate: each person for himself.

When Bao-wha with his friend finally reached the Christian and Missionary Alliance compound in Guilin, his parents sighed in relief and praised God. They were the last to complete the trek.

Another beginning

Professor Chang wasted no time. The Bible college had agreed to let them temporarily use an upper floor of their building. He gathered his little flock and seminary life resumed. Even in these circumstances, the Chang family had not ceased giving. Mother used her life savings to buy land and build a seminary. They received no outside help. To survive, they sold some of Mother's jewellery and their spare clothing and kitchen items at a roadside flea market. As Bao-wha sat on a small stool hawking their personal belongings, he could see small parts of his life slipping away.

He did not attend school, but sat in on some seminary classes.

Meanwhile the forces of Mao Zedong continued to press southward with the Nationalists fleeing before them in complete disarray. It became evident that the Communists would soon control all of mainland China. Indeed, by October of 1949, Chiang Kai-shek and the remnants of his army fled to Taiwan. Right across southern China, during the last years of the civil war, people who feared the Communists looked for ways to escape, triggering what would became a great Chinese dispersion. In western China, Nationalist deserters and those cut off from the main army drifted across frontiers into Burma, Laos, and Thailand. Many non-combatants chose to follow them, including great numbers of ethnic tribal peoples. To the east, refugees fled toward Taiwan and the British colony of Hong Kong.

Professor Chang faced a major decision. He called a family conference specifically for Bao-wha, a younger brother, Bao-yi, and an older sister, Bao-yun.

***

Bao-wha tensed as he sat with his brother and sister facing his parents. Three times he and his family had escaped the advancing communists. Would Father propose another move?

As though reading his son's mind, Professor Chang said,

"We will run no more. Mother and I have talked to your older married siblings; they have decided to stay as we will. Bao-yi and Bao-yun, will go to Taiwan to join Bao-cheng who is there now."

And what will I do? Bao-wha wondered.

His father wasn't finished, "Bao-wha, you have shown great promise for a career in the Christian ministry. You will go to Hong Kong to continue your studies. When you get there, Fred Savage or other CNEC people will see you get help."

"Do I travel alone?"

"Your brother and sister will travel with you as far as Hong Kong."

Bao-wha's mother spoke, "Remember the ring that I sewed into your jacket for the trip to Nanjing? It will travel with the three of you on this trip should you need to buy food."

In August of 1949, just two months before the complete collapse of the Nationalists, the three set out for Hong Kong. The train trip to Canton proved uneventful compared to Bao-wha's earlier adventures. The last leg of the journey to Hong Kong by junk, also successful, added a new travel dimension.

When they parted company in Hong Kong, Bao-yin took the ring, but Bao-wha kept another treasure. He had one copy of his father's book on personal evangelism. He dreamed that one day he would publish it in Hong Kong.

CHAPTER 6 *Education*

*Marcus Aurelius said, "Nothing befalls a man
except what is in his nature to endure."*

CNEC had grown since its early days and the original Sponsor-a-National concept. They had developed additional programs that later became known as Sponsor-a-Child and Sponsor-a-Student. Fred Savage looked for support for Bao-wha so he could continue his studies. An American woman, Mrs. Gladys Jackson who had supported Professor Chang, wanted to assist a pastor's child and supplied the necessary funds.

High school
Bao-wha's on-again, off-again studies meant he had to work hard to complete a high-school program—particularly when he could not understand the local dialect. He spoke Mandarin, the most popular language in northern China, but in the British colony the schools used Cantonese—a dialect of the south. Because Chinese writing uses pictographs rather than a phonetic alphabet, and all use the same symbols regardless of their dialect, they can read each other's writing. Bao-wha began his school experiences in Hong Kong by simply depending on the textbooks and communicating with written notes.

He made rapid progress learning Cantonese and soon became very busy. His years of musical experience and training under his sister, Bao-yin began to pay off. Not only did he begin voice lessons, but he led the choirs at the Living Water Christian Church, the Red Cliff Chapel, and the Christian Assembly Church. He also taught choir at the newly-formed Hong Kong Bible College.

Despite all the activity, or maybe because of it, Bao-wha found life difficult. Like many teenagers away from their families and friends, he did not always know what to do in demanding and exhausting circumstances. He experienced a crisis of faith during the four years of high school. When he finished high school in 1954, he had no thoughts on the future and no sense of call.

He sat alone in his room, a cloud of depression smothering his soul. He began arguing with himself—or maybe with God. *I feel like Cain, condemned to wander the face of the earth alone—without roots, without family.*

The times of fun and fellowship around the piano as a youngster played through his mind like an old newsreel, flickering and colourless. *Why, oh why can't those times come back. They seem so long ago. Oh dear God, I miss my family, my mother, my father.*

He could feel his mother's hugs and hear her prayers as though once again standing at the front door ready to flee the approaching Communists. In imagination he spoke to his mother, *Oh Mother how much you cared and prayed for me when we parted, and how you rejoiced when we all reunited safely at our destination. And my father, how I miss him too.*

The long talks he'd had with his father as they walked together on preaching tours came back with a clarity that surprised him, *I miss my father desperately. He always had the answer. He taught me so much—when we were alone, it was as if he had no other child, but I know he cared equally for all of us. Oh, I wish I could see him again.*

Bao-wha leaped to his feet and spoke aloud to the empty room, "That's it! I'll return to China. I'll visit my father and ask for his advice. Maybe China isn't as bad as they say. Maybe I'll stay there near my family."

Flirting with communism

Bao-wha encountered no problems re-entering China. The Chinese authorities seemed to welcome the return of one who might be a repentant citizen, but they stopped his progress toward Guilin when he reached Canton, now Guangzhou. Unable to continue, he spent two weeks observing life under communism. While walking the streets of Canton, he observed the people, noting that the plainness and uniformity of their clothes extended to their faces. When he talked to them, they seemed to resent his intrusion. He saw no beggars on the street.

The people looked well fed, but without spirit or excitement in their lives.

No way! Bao-wha thought. *I could never live here. There is no freedom to travel, not even freedom to think.*

He pulled out his papers and examined them—his refugee documents from Hong Kong would take him back to a land of freedom. Tucking them carefully back into a secure inner pocket, he turned about and headed for the hostel to collect his things. He would return to Hong Kong immediately—if the local authorities would grant him exit papers. To his surprise and pleasure the officials stamped his papers and waved him through.

A stream of people flowed steadily toward the Hong Kong immigration gates, but the authorities seemed to turn back as many as they passed through. Bao-wha fingering his papers, thought, *Thank God I got in four years ago. It's much harder to get out of China today.*

When his turn came, he placed his papers on the counter and smiled at the official. The man scowled back, shoved the papers back to him, and said, "This refugee permit is invalid. You must have a current travel document and a visa to enter Hong Kong."

"But I left Hong Kong just days ago."

"No matter. Get the proper papers and come back. Next please."

Bao-wha waited until he could try again with another official, but he got the same curt answers. Five times he approached the officials—he argued and begged—but five times they turned him away. For the sixth time he approached the entry point desperately looking for a way in. As the line grew shorter he saw a tall police officer. He studied him for a moment, then guessed he was a native of Shandong. The police department of Hong Kong preferred tall men and often chose Shandong natives. In fact Bao-wha had a relative on the force, badge number 2980.

He approached the policeman, briefly blurted out his story, and said, "I'm a relative of Officer 2980."

"What's his name?"

Speaking quietly and using conspiratorial tones, Bao-wha told him.

"Follow me," the policeman said.

Within minutes they sped past the British officers and safely into Hong Kong territory.

College

Back in Hong Kong, shaken by his experience, and feeling God wanted to tell him something, Bao-wha fell on his knees, *Lord, what do you want me to do?*

The answer came, not through a stunning revelation or by an audible voice from heaven, but through a certainty within his heart. He applied for entrance to Hong Kong's Bethel Bible Seminary, they accepted him, and he began a four-year program.

One day at a church service, he saw a familiar face, a familiar figure, an American missionary with the China Inland Mission.[32] He greeted him, "Reverend Russell Glazer! Good afternoon sir."

The missionary stared blankly at Bao-wha.

"I'm Chang Bao-wha, son of Chang Hsueh Kung. We met in Nanjing."

Glazer's eyes lit up and he caught Bao-wha by the arm. "Bao-wha, so good to see you. Let's go for a walk and talk about old times. And you can tell me about yourself."

To one so young the expression *old times* sounded inappropriate, but then China and life in general had changed drastically since those heady days in Nanjing.

The two walked for a while then sat cross-legged at the roadside to exchange stories. Glancing down, Bao-wha's eyes fell on Glazer's shoes—he saw a hole in the sole, a hole lined with newspapers. Surprise shifted Bao-wha's attention from the conversation. He thought, *How can this be? Aren't all missionaries rich?*

Noting Bao-wha's change of focus, Glazer said, "Yes I need new shoes. When the Lord provides the funds, I'll buy a new pair. I walked in these shoes all the way from Shanghai to escape the Communists."

Bao-wha sat quietly, a new appreciation of missionaries dawning on him.

Glazer continued speaking, "I have given my whole life to China. I am now Chinese on the inside and American on the outside. When I die, I want my body buried in China."

That encounter left Bao-wha with an overpowering sense that God had spoken to him through the missionary. He knew now with absolute certainty that God had called him to full-time missionary service.

Bao-wha threw himself into his studies. He became pastor of Red Cliff Chapel and organized gospel teams to minister in Hong Kong's New Territories. He made another move that would greatly influence his musical life. He took lessons from the voice teacher, Dr. Theodore Huang from whom he learned proper voice production and choir conducting. Dr. Huang had studied at the prestigious Westminster Choir School in Princeton, New Jersey.

Early in 1958 Bao-wha received a letter from his father. It said in part, "They have taken everything. I am in Manchuria, living apart from the family. Your mother is well and staying with your brother in Guilin."

The letter seemed vague, almost evasive. Did his father, cautious lest a government censor read it, hope he would understand an implied message? The letter included two Scripture verses: "Therefore, strengthen your feeble arms and weak knees"[33] and "But the Lord stood at my side and gave me strength so that through me the message might be fully proclaimed and all the gentiles might hear it."

The letter also said, "Even though my arms are so heavy, I still raise them up in God's service."

As Bao-wha held the letter, he realized that even though the Communist government had censured his father, no amount of suffering would prevent him from preaching the gospel. He could not know of the events then transpiring in China. The government asked his father to join the Three-Self Church[35] and become the principal of Kim Ling Theological Seminary. When he refused, they revoked his citizenship, making him homeless—his only alternative was to become an itinerant preacher. Many other pastors found themselves in the same position. Neither could Bao-wha know that he would receive no more letters from his father.

Only years later would Bao-wha learn all the facts and understand that his father's persecution, and that of other itinerant preachers, had given birth to China's great house-church movement.

Bao-wha graduated from Bethel in 1958 with a Bachelor of Theology degree and looked about for life's next challenge. Should he accept a position in ministry with a church in Hong Kong? Should he continue his education? If so where? His father had studied in the United States of America. He had a good friend from Hong Kong studying at Seattle Pacific College.[36] A smile spread across Bao-wha's face. He thought, *Seattle Pacific has a great music program!*

CNEC, as a matter of policy, would not sponsor nationals for study overseas. They had experienced disappointments when nationals had refused to return home after completing their studies.[37] If Bao-wha wished to study overseas, he would be on his own, but CNEC would offer encouragement and moral support. Bao-wha approached Cecil Kettle—one of the five original founding members of the CNEC board, and then president of the United States council—asking for a letter that might help him get overseas to study. Kettle knew Bao-wha's father very well and stretched the rules to the limit by providing a letter that vaguely guaranteed his stay while in the States. Kettle used a letterhead that displayed a list of the companies in which he held directorships.

Introducing Paul Chang

Many of Bao-wha's friends who had gone overseas for study, or who worked with Westerners, had adopted western or Christian names—almost a necessity around English-speaking people who typically stumbled over Chinese names. He toyed with the Chinese rendering of the name for the Apostle Paul: Bao-luo. *Bao-luo—Bao-wha. It does sound something like my name,* he thought.

He felt a flutter of emotion run through his body, but his hand remained firm as he wrote the name for the first time. On the application form for a visa to the United States of America, in the space for family name, he wrote *Chang*, but on the line for given name, he wrote *Paul*. So with the stroke of a pen Chang Bao-wha became Paul Chang—at least to his Western friends.

In the United States embassy in Hong Kong, the official locked eyes with the young man and said, "Mr. Chang, we must have a four hundred dollar deposit before we can give you a visa to enter the States."

"I don't have it," Bao-wha come Paul answered.

A note of suspicion crept into the official's voice, "Are your parents in China? Will you return to China?"

Not sure how to answer, Paul said, "Does this help?" and pushed Cecil Kettle's letter across the desk.

The official read the letter, then remained silent for a full minute while he studied the list of directorships of well-known American companies. Obviously impressed, he stamped the visa application.

Paul left the embassy with a silent prayer of thanks to the Lord. He now had a visa and one hundred dollars in the bank. But he also had a request: *Lord, you have given me the visa. Now I need two hundred dollars more.*

The Lord provided and Paul embarked on his American adventure, financed by the grand sum of three hundred dollars. A third-class ticket to San Francisco on the steamship, *President Wilson*, cost two hundred, seventy dollars. He would have thirty dollars in his pocket. His "cabin" aboard the ship—really just a large room—accommodated 20 people. But what luxury for one whose previous travels had included pushing a handcart through the snow, clinging to the outside of a train, and squeezing into overcrowded ferries or junks.

On board the ship he met many other Christians and students—some bound on similar ventures. Arriving in San Francisco he faced an additional journey to Seattle—a distance of over one thousand three hundred kilometres. The bus ticket cost him twenty-three dollars—he'd have little left for meals. But again the Lord provided: an affluent Hong Kong student, also headed for Seattle, bought him food. With little more that change in his pocket he arrived on campus on Monday with school starting on Tuesday.

Surviving in America

Paul knew the school provided working scholarships, but he also knew two hundred, seventy dollars for tuition for the first semester would come due on Tuesday. On Tuesday Paul faced the registrar and filled out the forms. When he came to the line asking for the money, his body tensed. Would the Lord let him get this far and not provide the fees?

"I don't have the money," he said.

"No problem," the registrar answered. "Just sign your name."

Paul found himself quickly swept into life on campus and caught up in American culture. That very day, a female student hailed him. "Paul Chang?"

He turned to face her, "Yes, I'm Chang Bao-. . ., Paul Chang."

She introduced herself, and said, "News travels fast. I've heard you have a great tenor voice."

"I do sing," Paul replied with a slight hesitation.

"I'm responsible for the music for vespers Wednesday night, tomorrow night. I'd like you to sing a solo."

"I'd be happy to do that," he responded.

Paul made his American singing debut at the Wednesday night vespers service in the college chapel by singing, *His Eye is on the Sparrow*.

Following vespers as he exited backstage, a beautiful blonde American girl approached him and asked him if he would be her date at the Sadie Hawkins' Day party.

On Thursday when exploring the bulletin board, he saw an announcement by the United Evangelical Free Church—they wanted a choir conductor. Overcoming a hesitancy that should accompany anyone who had just entered a new country with an alien culture and a language he barely spoke, he applied. They asked him to sing on Sunday. Following his song and an interview, they hired him as choir director for seventy dollars per month.

Work and school

Paul's first week at college foreshadowed the pattern that would follow him throughout his four years at Seattle Pacific College. He continued to lead the choir. He needed more money so took a job as a janitor. For four hours each weekday, he cleaned toilets and removed the grime left behind by others. On Friday night and Saturday he worked as a busboy for a Chinese restaurant. Although he earned only minimum wage, the job had other advantages—the restaurant gave him two meals each day he worked and allowed him to take leftovers back to school. During holidays he worked eight hours a day for less than one dollar an hour. To speed him to the various activities, Paul purchased a 1953 Chevrolet for three hundred dollars.

In the early months at the college, Paul faced a challenge not experienced by most students. He spoke Mandarin and Cantonese and adequate English to carry on basic conversations, but not nearly enough to fully participate in college classes. Improving his English became a daily on-the-job process.

One sour note entered Paul's life in 1960. The news arrived from China that his father had died in a Chinese prison on March the 5th of that year.

Music remained central to Paul's life. He immersed himself in the college's music program, performing for three years in the a cappella choir and accepting invitations to sing for churches. Occasionally this meant school and personal ministry tours. On one of those trips to California in 1961 he met Allen Finley, the new executive director of CNEC. During his orientation, Finley had heard much about Professor Chang Hsueh Kung and appreciated the opportunity to meet his son. That meeting would have far-reaching consequences.

To add another dimension to his busyness, three Mandarin-speaking families asked Paul to minister to them. He took the challenge, but involved other students. The small group eventually became a church, later developing into one of the fastest growing in Seattle.

Paul Chang graduated from Seattle Pacific College with a Bachelor of Arts degree in 1962.

The months following graduation became a pattern for many summers to follow. Allen Finley asked him to do deputation work for CNEC during that summer—to tell churches about the work of the organization. What better person could Finley find than the son of one of the original CNEC missionaries, and one who had received support himself during his student days in Hong Kong.

CNEC supplied a car, a Nash Rambler. Paul got an Ampex reel-to-reel tape recorder to play the accompaniment for his solos and hit the road. At churches and other venues where Finley could arrange meetings, Paul sang and gave his personal testimony. The commendations flooded back to the CNEC office and other churches opened their doors.

The summer of 1962 introduced another great benefit for Paul—Allen Finley became his mentor, and Allen and his wife Ruth became Paul's lifelong friends.

Graduate school

With music as a major focus in his ministry, Paul looked for an appropriate graduate school in an area near a large Chinese population. He chose Golden Gate Baptist Theological Seminary in the San Francisco Bay area and began classes in the fall of 1962, majoring in both church music and Christian education. A double major would have kept most people busy, but Paul made room for Christian ministry.

Almost immediately, he accepted a position as music director at the Oakland Evangelical Free Church where he stayed until early 1964. In the summer of 1964 the Chinese Cumberland Presbyterian Church asked him to become youth director and choir director. Late in 1964 he became music and youth director at Oakland Chinese Independent Baptist Church.[38] He stayed there until the end of 1965.

All of these churches contributed to Paul's experience and development, but the summer at Cumberland Presbyterian changed his life forever.

The pianist at Cumberland chose the summer of 1964 to get married, not knowing his honeymoon would trigger major events in the lives of two other people. He arranged for Liu Nien-chang to take his place at the piano. It didn't take Paul long to realize he had much in common with this petite, pretty young lady. She too had grown up in China and fled before the Japanese and communists. She too had come to America, in her case becoming an American citizen, studying at Hunter College, then earning a master's degree in nutrition at Cornell.

He also learned she worked as a dietician doing research on the relationships between diet and heart disease. But there was one thing he didn't ask and didn't know.

They saw each other every weekend. By the summer's end, only three to four months after meeting, the smitten choir director proposed to the substitute pianist. She accepted, and only then did Paul learn the detail that Nien-chang had held back.

His future bride was the daughter of the Taiwan ambassador to Thailand. Her father had a distinguished career with the foreign service of the Chinese Nationalist government, beginning in Nanjing before the Nationalists fled to Taiwan. He had served in Korea, at the United Nations in New York, in Cuba, and then in Thailand. Mr. Liu had moved his family to the United States during his time with the UN.

They married on January 23, 1965. In May of that year Paul graduated with a master's degree in church music (M.C.M.) and a master's in religious education (M.R.E.).

During Paul's time at seminary, he also studied under a noted California voice teacher, Mrs. McMurray, who in her earlier career had sung with Caruso. Although in her nineties, she still carried a heavy load of voice students. McMurray saw potential in Paul and offered to get him a position with the San Francisco Operatic Society. He refused; he could think of nothing but returning to Hong Kong and a career in ministry. But before he could do that, he still faced an informal time of training.

The first half of 1965 had proven full and exciting for the new-lyweds, but the second half set the tone for the rest of their lives. In October of that year, Paul accepted an offer from Allen Finley to join CNEC to do full-time deputation work and on November 17, Nien-chang gave birth to a boy. They called him Mark.[39]

CHAPTER 7: *Life on the Road*

*Augustine said, "The world is a book, and
those who do not travel, read only one page."*

Paul had already experienced travel, most often under difficult
circumstances. Now CNEC offered him the chance to read many
more of the world's pages.

The deputation trail

Within days of the birth of his son, Paul embarked on his first
major deputation tour to the southeastern United States with his
first stop in French Camp, about an hour and a half northeast of
Jackson, Mississippi. Of course Paul wasn't beginning the journey in Jackson—he had to drive there from California!

With the thoughts of a three-month tour ahead of him, separated from his wife and new baby, Paul almost quit. Somehow,
he managed to persevere—after all his father had spent much
more time apart from his mother.

Once on site he met up with the area representative of CNEC,
Fred Manning.[40] Manning kept him busy visiting congregations
of a Presbyterian group of churches.[41] They received Paul enthusiastically, responding well to his music and testimony. Many
began supporting him financially through CNEC.[42]

Paul survived that first trip and returned home to Oakland
early in 1966. Soon he set out on more tours, sometimes taking
Nien-chang and the baby with him. At every meeting or church
service, he sang, quickly earning himself the nickname: *Chinese
Singing Ambassador.* Somewhere during that hectic year, a
question began circulating in the minds of Paul and Allen
Finley—*Why not produce a record?*

"Paul," asked Allen one evening at a casual meeting that
included one board member, "Why don't you make an album of
your most popular songs?"

"I've thought about it, but who would we get to record it?
And could we afford it?"

"I think we can answer those questions," Allen said.

The album that won't go away

Paul Chang's album became a great success—not only as a technique for raising funds, but as a ministry. The Reverend John G. Pearce, a retired Anglican minister approached the author, Ray Wiseman, during a book tour to Nova Scotia, Canada, in 1999. He looked at a copy of *Disciples of Joy* and noted the publisher's name.

"Is that the organization that once went by the name CNEC?" he asked.

"Yes."

"Does Paul Chang still work with you?"

"He certainly does."

A smile crept slowly across his face, "Some time back, maybe 20 or 25 years ago, a minister friend from another denomination invited me to hear him. I thoroughly enjoyed his singing and testimony and bought his record. I still enjoy listening to it today."

Paul has even better stories about that vinyl disk.

A lady asked to see Paul during a deputation trip to Scotland. She arrived carrying a copy of the record. "I just wanted to thank you for making this record. It saved my life."

"Tell me about it," Paul said.

"A friend who lives in New Zealand sent it to me. Soon after receiving it, I went through a terrible time of depression. I got to the point of deciding to commit suicide. But, thank God, I began listening to your record. I listened to it for two weeks. The message of the hymns got through to my heart and soul and the depression lifted. The record saved my life!"

In 1969 Paul made a deputation trip to Perth, Australia. Twenty years later he returned and visited one of the same churches. At the church a man approached him and said, "Paul, I need to tell you this. Your record saved my life."

Have I heard this story before? Paul asked himself, but aloud he said, "Tell me about it."

"When you came to our church years ago, I bought your record. I had gone bankrupt and considered committing suicide, but listening to your record brought me through that difficult time."

The board member shook his head, "No! It's a waste of time. We're in the business of raising funds to support national workers. We're not in the record business."

"I do believe we need to give it some thought," answered Allen.

In fact Allen had a vision and wouldn't allow the opinion of one board member to shake him. He pressed ahead, and using the knowledge and influence of various members of the CNEC board, engaged Paul Mickelson of the Billy Graham organization to produce it using the Lawrence Whitney studio. They booked it for three three-hour recording sessions.

One day in 1967 Paul arrived at the studio with no practice—with his busy life, when would he find time to rehearse? And did one who sang publicly almost daily need practice? They completed the album in one three-hour session and issued *Paul Chang, Chinese Singing Ambassador*.

Allen pushed ahead with his dream. CNEC had received a request from Hong Kong to help finance a new high school. He arranged a matching grant. For each dollar raised by sales of the record, a major donor would provide an additional dollar. The record left the office in great numbers. Paul sold them by the boxful wherever he went. Eventually they moved about 15,000 at a profit of approximately six dollars each.

The missionary vision
The year 1967 proved a great year for Paul Chang in many ways. Allen Finley asked him to visit some of the fields so he could better represent them while on deputation work. The trip took Paul to Hong Kong, Malaysia, and Thailand. Thailand had the greatest impact on Paul; there he got a first-hand picture of life on a mission frontier. He found northern Thailand extremely backward. They had no public transportation so he rode on the back of a truck, usually sitting on a bag of rice. He arrived at most destinations covered with dust from the dirt roads, dust that penetrated to the skin.

Something else penetrated even deeper than the skin. Paul returned home with an enhanced missionary vision. He knew now he would return to southeast Asia to become personally involved in missionary work.

The stork lands again

The latter half of the year found Paul, Nien-chang, and Mark, now a toddler, on another tour to the southeastern United States. Even though Paul tried to ease the burden of the trip for Nien-chang's sake—she was six months pregnant—he still found himself in a whirl of activity.

On Sunday they ministered at a Presbyterian church in Birmingham, Alabama. On Monday Paul left Nien-chang and Mark with friends in Birmingham and drove three hours to Atlanta, Georgia, to hold a meeting at a Baptist church.

The pastor met with Paul before the service began. In the course of the orientation the pastor said, "You should know that we don't support Billy Graham at this church."

Fully aware of the movement that had grown among certain evangelical churches with fundamentalist leanings, Paul thought quickly. They rejected the ministry of Billy Graham, classifying him as a neo-evangelical, because he cooperated with all churches, including those with liberal theology. A wrong reaction to the pastor's comment could prevent Paul from speaking at the church; it could jeopardize the entire ministry of CNEC among similar churches should they think of CNEC as neo-evangelical.

Paul could give but one answer, the truth. "Well, I support the ministry of Billy Graham because he held a crusade in Hong Kong and the church received much blessing."

The sky didn't fall; the church didn't collapse around him. The pastor simply nodded and they proceeded to plan the meeting. That evening Paul ministered, the people received him well, and the church became a long-term supporter.

On Tuesday before Paul could move on, he received a phone call. A tense voice blurted out the message, "Paul, Nien-chang is in the hospital with a hemorrhage. The doctors feel she will lose the baby, but they will try to save it."

The next day—Wednesday, November 29, 1967—Paul

returned to Birmingham and visited Nien-chang at West End Baptist Hospital. That evening he kept an appointment to speak at a prayer meeting. Following the meeting, he rushed back to the hospital, but discovered that someone else had arrived ahead of him—his new daughter, weighing in at 2.5 pounds.[43] They called her Ruth.[44] When the first waves of joy and thankfulness created by the miracle baby's birth had subsided, Paul and Nien-chang began considering the challenges before them. How do they return to California with a premature baby? Should they cancel the remainder of the tour? Should they stay in the area for a few weeks?

A hospital official answered most of their questions by saying, "We must keep her here until she reaches five or six pounds."

Within a few days they continued the tour, moving on to Florida, but calling the hospital every day for a progress report. After two months they picked up Ruthie, and the family of four hit the road for California. The hospital bills for such a stay would have severely strained the average family in those days before most people carried health insurance. But no one could call the Changs average—they had little money and few physical possessions beyond the clothes they wore.

Back in California at the CNEC office, Allen and Ruth Finley had quickly spread the news of the Chang's plight. By the time friends and supporters had pitched in, Paul had to pay a mere four hundred dollars. In Paul's words, "The Lord provided!"

The deputation game
During those busy years, Paul made seven trips across the United States and Canada. Sometimes he travelled alone; sometimes he took Nien-chang and the children. All, who have travelled long distances by car with a family, know how it affects children. They enjoy the adventure of the first day on the road. By the second or third day they become so agitated travel becomes difficult if not impossible for children and parents.

The Changs developed a travel plan that made life bearable. On a typical long trip, they loaded Mark and Ruthie into the back seat of the car at three o'clock in the morning. The children, barely wakened by the shift in beds, would continue to sleep for about five hours while the car made good progress.

When the kids awoke, the parents got a break from the wheel and everyone ate breakfast. Often at meal times they would find a park with metered electricity and cook a meal in a rice cooker. Typically they would check into a motel at three o'clock and prepare the evening meal—then off to bed early and on the road again at three in the morning.

A missionary kid's viewpoint

Mark Chang recalls those long-distance car trips: "As a family, we were never in need of anything. I remember how, during one of our many trips across the U.S. for deputation, we would eat lettuce, a can of luncheon meat, and rice (the rice cooker: never leave home without it). But my parents never complained. We got our clothes and toys out of the missionary barrel. As kids, I don't think we complained either, because our parents didn't—and they instilled in us the sense of God's providence."

Paul and Nien-chang's travel and eating habits differed so much from other CNEC representatives, they often got questioned at the office when they turned in expense accounts. After examining the figures and noting a lack of restaurant charges, a secretary would ask, "Don't you guys ever eat when you're on the road?"

Doing deputation work results in times of great blessing, but it also has moments of weariness and disappointment.

On one occasion Paul drove alone, non-stop, all the way from California to Arkansas, arriving late at the church. The pastor ushered him right in. Paul sang and preached, but he was so tired he had to lean against the pulpit. At the end of the service, the pastor took up an offering for the missionaries supported by the church, and gave Paul ten dollars for his effort.

At the next church things turned out differently. Again Paul did his very best, this time without the hindrance of extreme tiredness. When the pastor made an appeal to the congregation, the people responded, assuming the sponsorship of 30 children. When you multiply the yearly support figure for each child times 30, and realize that most sponsors continue their support for many years, that meeting resulted in multitudes of thousands of dollars flowing to needy children around the world.

Unfortunately, even in churches, race influences the attitudes of some people. At one church a particularly sour looking matron glared at Paul as he entered and said, "What is that Mongolian doing here?"

Unshaken by her comment, Paul proceeded with his part in the program, but he kept his eye on the disparager. As the service progressed, he watched her face soften. Paul later said, "I watched her heart melt as I sang and preached."

Paul had a knack of arriving in the right place at the right time and meeting key people. Bible Town in Florida, asked Paul to take part in their first missionary conference. They had also invited Oswald J. Smith, founder of The Peoples Church in Toronto, to come as keynote speaker. At that time Peoples had already become noted for its missionary program and large yearly budget for support of missionaries. In 1959, Smith had transferred the pastorate of Peoples Church to his son, Paul B. Smith, but had retained responsibility for the missions' program.

Smith, revered as a great missionary statesman, had never taken kindly to the concept of money from "foreign" or Western churches going to national workers. Indeed he wrote:

> The work should be *self-supporting, self-governing,* and *self-propagating,* and that from the first. No one can be healthy and strong while leaning on another. Churches have become weak and indolent rather than aggressive and powerful as a result of foreign support.[45]

Paul took half of the musical segments for the conference, with other well-known Christian musicians performing the rest. Oswald. J. Smith obviously noticed him, for he extended an invitation to Paul to attend a mission's conference at Peoples Church. Paul already had an "in" at Peoples Church. When Pastor Paul B. Smith had preached in Hong Kong in 1954, a student by the name of Paul Chang had acted as song leader and interpreter.

Times and opinions change. Paul did visit the mission's conference at Peoples Church and became their first national Christian worker to receive support.

Paul Smith later referred to Paul Chang as his million-dollar man because the church first exceeded the one million dollar mark during a mission conference that featured Paul.

John Kao, a friend of Paul's from Hong Kong days, also came to North America and accepted a position raising funds for CNEC. Paul and John made a deputation trip to Briarwood Presbyterian Church in Birmingham, Alabama, a church founded by Frank Bakker. Pastor Bakker warned them, "We're going to be busy. I'm going to work you fellows to death!"

He kept his word—well, almost! He planned a whirl of activity, arranging a round of meetings, so that they ministered to a different group every day. The church had started in a school and had grown quickly. John Kao, impressed by the organization of the church, took careful note of everything. Possibly, one day, he could use the Briarwood model should he ever plant a church.[46]

Map of Southeast Asia

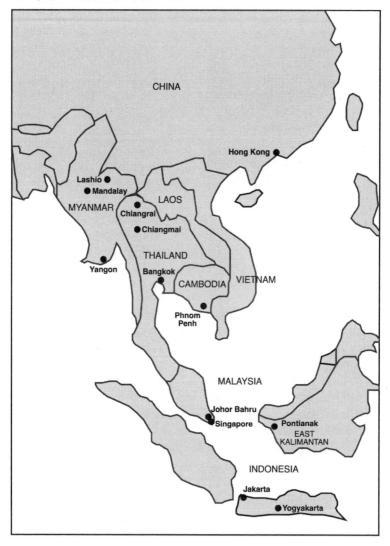

PART 3: BUILDING BRIDGES

*If you do not walk in their footsteps, you do not gain
access to their abode.*
—Confucius

*God moves in a mysterious way
His wonders to perform;
He plants his footsteps in the sea,
And rides upon the storm.*
—William Cowper

Where there is no vision, the people perish.
—Proverbs 28:18

CHAPTER 8: *Return to Asia*

"Mist wreathed the green dragon hills of China and clung to the stern granite crest that dominated the island. Birds called from the depths of hidden valleys, and blue bays with crescents of sand welcomed the travel-worn voyagers."[47]

In the above quote, Trea Wiltshire describes the arrival of missionary nuns in Hong Kong harbour in the 1840s. When Paul Chang returned there as a missionary, a different vista greeted him: all the signs of industry and commerce in a modern city of skyscrapers teeming with needy people.

Difficult times in Hong Kong

In 1970 Paul accepted an assignment from CNEC to join their ministries in Hong Kong, taking the position as understudy to Dr. Andrew Song who planned to retire. Paul, Nien-chang, and the children moved into an apartment previously vacated by Arthur Gee who had served in Hong Kong and moved to Singapore to head the CNEC field office there.

Back in Hong Kong Paul reconnected with old friends. When he had taught Sunday School in CNEC Redcliff Chapel prior to going to the States, Cheung Sau-ming (Esther) had attended as a preteen. Now on his return, she worked in the CNEC field office under Paul's direction. Esther and Paul's ministries would continue to interact for years to come.

Paul soon found himself in a whirl of activity. He taught church music and Christian education in the Hong Kong Bible Seminary and accepted responsibility for the CNEC youth ministry. His position as associate field director also gave him oversight of the three CNEC churches in Taiwan, which dictated that he fly there every three months. For the first time in his life Paul found himself in a key leadership position with pressures coming from all directions. He had never experienced serious problems with interpersonal relationships, but now he found himself in a whole new world—tensions began to build between him and some pastors. They knew he had come to replace Dr.

Song and, thinking him too young or inexperienced, they acted toward him with suspicion and, at times, jealousy.

Paul had no problem moving back to a Chinese dominated society, but he didn't like certain negative elements he now faced. Ingredients of the old China, for centuries ridden with favouritism and corruption, tainted Hong Kong society—indeed, it had even crept into the Church. CNEC, reacting to a need, had established schools on the roofs of apartment buildings in resettlement areas—districts where the continuing stream of refugees from China settled. CNEC accepted subsidies from the government of Hong Kong to defray operating costs, to the extent that the school income became an important part of their budget. Opportunists, hoping for personal gain, began coming to Paul, offering gifts and seeking positions in the schools. Paul saw the gifts as bribes and refused to accept them.

During Chinese New Year, an age-old custom dictates that married people give red envelopes containing money to unmarried people. A few began giving money to Paul's children—perfectly acceptable within reason. But when Paul realized they were doing it to curry favour and get profitable or influential positions in schools, churches or related ministries, he condemned the practice. One person seriously distorted the red-envelope custom by giving Ruth a gold chain. Paul reacted to this and other blatant displays of simony[48] by rejecting the requests for personal favour and returning excessive gifts.

All this confused the Chang children who could not differentiate between acceptable and unacceptable gifts. Paul and Nien-chang tried to help Mark and Ruth by explaining the custom. "Not everyone will give you gifts. Only people who know you well, and only married people, should ever give you red envelopes containing money. According to the custom, unmarried people don't give money."

Mark, aged four, tucked away his father's words and waited for an opportunity to test his new knowledge. A few days later, the seminary president and his wife came for a visit. Mark waited patiently, but the visitor gave out no red envelopes. Mark sidled up to him, ignoring the wife who sat beside her husband.

Pulling on his shirt, he looked up into the respected man's face and asked, "Are you married?"

The Hong Kong leadership appointed Paul as an assistant to Dr. Song. In this position, he became responsible for church planting and immediately sensed another problem. The churches depended on overseas funding for salaries; the situation hadn't changed much since the earliest days of CNEC in Hong Kong, but it ran contrary to the organization's basic principles. The local churches had not caught the vision of becoming self-supporting; they had not developed a missionary vision, robbing themselves of opportunities to become a blessing to others and consequently stunting their own growth—they lived in a culture of dependency.

Paul did not take long to make a momentous ruling. He applied the same practical logic he used in personal decision-making: analyze the circumstances; ask God for direction; arrive at answers that please God even if they cause personal sacrifice and don't always draw the applause of men; then, let God work out the application in his way.

He announced the new policy to the pastors and church workers: "It's time the churches become fully self-supporting. We will cut the CNEC contributions to salaries by 50 per cent next year, and eliminate them totally by the following year."

Paul's decision shook the CNEC structure in Hong Kong. It annoyed many; only a few saw it as an opportunity for growth.

Paul saw gift-giving or bribery, and dependence on government and overseas money, as serious problems that impeded the development of the Hong Kong churches. Even some students attended Bible college strictly as a career opportunity, as an easy living. And why not? CNEC paid their fees and living expenses while at school and a salary when they later took a CNEC position.

Paul cast about for answers to the problems and decided to lead by example. He made a bold move: Nien-chang and he, with help from a number of students, started a new church, named the Kowloon Church. Esther chose to join the team, as did Simon Fan, a student at the Baptist college who worked part time under Paul's direction at the CNEC student centre.

Beginning with seven students, they concentrated on family and Sunday school. Nien-chang taught children's classes, later switching to adults. Paul began a basketball outreach program to attract young people. In the first year the church grew to one hundred people; in the second year they held a mission conference with John Kao as the featured speaker. Years later, the church changed its name to the CNEC Fellowship Church, and became the largest CNEC church in Hong Kong.[49]

During the Chang family's Hong Kong sojourn, Paul continued his involvement in music. He became tenor soloist for the oratorical society, did a TV series on baroque music, led choirs and continued to teach voice to students, including Esther. Some of those students, and others who came up through the basketball program, eventually emigrated to Canada and became involved in the church-planting ministry of Dr. John Kao.

In 1974 Paul filled an important role at a wedding. When Esther Cheung[50] married Simon Fan,[51] Paul gave away the bride.

Lausanne and beyond

The Lausanne Conference on World Evangelization in 1974 changed the face of many mission organizations around the world. On that occasion Dr. Ralph Winter contended that mission agencies had neglected groups of people by failing to establish among them culturally relevant, viable, churches. This earned him the reputation as the "father of the unreached-peoples movement."[52] Like numerous other organizations CNEC leadership and many of their partner ministries caught the vision of establishing programs to target people previously neglected or under-evangelized.

CNEC asked Paul to move to Singapore to temporarily replace Art Gee who had gone to the United States to do deputation work for a year. Paul accepted it as an opportunity to leave behind the tensions of Hong Kong and as a chance to evaluate his leadership style, for even he accepted that his choleric personality had contributed to the stresses of his term there.

Although ostensibly an interim appointment, Paul saw Singapore as an opportunity to establish new and reinforce existing ministries in that area. He responded with enthusiasm and moved his family to Singapore in August of 1974—he felt his time in Hong Kong had strengthened and prepared him for what lay ahead.

The CNEC Southeast Asia office had opened in Singapore in the early 1950s. John Lu led it for years, prior to Arthur Gee.

Nien-chang regretted leaving the church they had been part of since its inception; she would miss many new friends, but she too looked forward to new challenges.

Soon after settling in, Paul planned a trip to West Kalimantan[53] in Indonesia to inspect the work there. He had to prepare himself for a totally new approach to ministry—no longer would he travel the roads of America in a comfortable car, or minister among urbanized Chinese people living in the congested apartment towers of Hong Kong. He would come face-to-face with rural Chinese folk and tribal people who could only dream of the advantages and comforts of civilization, who often lacked the basic necessities of life like clean water and schools.

He would have to learn new customs. Co-workers with experience warned him of cultural differences. They explained that the tribal people reserved their left hands for dirty tasks, using only their right hands for clean things such as eating and making contact with people. "So, Paul," they said, "never use your left hand for those tasks or you will insult them."

Paul had a sense of trepidation as he looked at his hands. Truly, each hand was a mirror image of the other and should do whatever the owner asked, but he knew not every person could change easily from left to right. "I'm in trouble," he responded, "I'm left-handed."

No regular airline flights connected Singapore with West Kalimantan, so he booked a seat on a small charter turboprop that took him to Pontianak, the major city in the Indonesian province. Arriving safely, he boarded an 18 seat bus laden down with 30 passengers and their goods and headed for Sanggau. The enterprising owners had placed boards between the seats to accommodate extra passengers and had packed four or five people into the driver's compartment. The driver had to sit sideways! A roof rack bulged with the passengers' luggage and freight items, making the bus decidedly top-heavy.

The vehicle stopped along the roadside so the passengers could buy food from hawkers who offered a variety of choices. Flies swarmed about the crude kitchens and dirty cooking pots, causing Paul's stomach to churn. As he surveyed the less-than-appetizing choices, he remembered the wise counsel he had heard from experienced missionaries: "Eat only what you can boil or peel." He settled for steamed rice, salted eggs, and bananas, making that his standard fare for the rest of the journey.

Arriving at the church tired and dirty, Paul saw a large mud hole in front of the building. When he asked about getting a bath or shower, the church workers suggested he do so by bailing water from the mud hole. Facilities looked better along the river. There the people had built huts on anchored rafts. The huts had a toilet at one end and a place to bathe or wash clothes at the other. Paul could not help but wonder whether people cared if water drawn for bathing might have become contaminated by an upstream toilet.

But he had not come to West Kalimantan for a luxurious holiday—he had come to minister, and minister he did—three thousand people, mostly ethnic Chinese and Dayaks came to hear him preach.

More Chinese people lived in West Kalimantan than in other parts of Indonesia—about 15 per cent compared with 5 per cent in the rest of the country. About 40 per cent of the people in Kalimantan come from Indonesian/Malaysian parentage, while the Dayaks, a tribal group, also make up about 40 percent. History records that Chinese traders had established posts in the Pontianak area as long ago as AD 1000.[54] The majority of Chinese people in West Kalimantan speak the Hakka dialect. Relationships between Chinese and Dayaks had not always gone well. In 1967 for political reasons, elements of Indonesia's Muslim community provoked the Dayaks to rise up against the

Chinese. Many of them fled to Pontianak and settled in Kota Baru, a refugee camp, formerly a sawdust dump for the lumber industry. CNEC started a work among them in 1970.

The Chinese had faced and survived a much earlier attempt at racial cleansing. During the war, Japanese soldiers rounded them up, took them to isolated places and killed them by the truckload. In an attempt to atone for that massacre a Japanese businessman much later built a memorial in their memory.

From the mostly-Chinese community, Paul travelled on to visit a Dayak village. The roads, nothing more than paths, could not support buses. Paul found himself clinging to the back of a motorcycle. Three times the metal steed struck uneven ground or mud and pitched the driver and reluctant passenger into the dirt. They arrived uninjured except for minor bruises.

Paul found himself in a culture radically different from anything he had experienced among his countrymen. The Dayak tribal people lived in long houses built on poles over the river. A wooden gangway gave access to the front; boats could pull up behind or under the houses. Litter cluttered the shore and floated in the water under the flimsy buildings.

Other elements of Dayak lifestyle surprised Paul even more. He learned that persons experiencing a bad mood would close their doors and hang a leaf that symbolically said, "Stay out!" Human skulls hung from many houses, indicating that some people had faced situations far more serious than a neighbour in a foul mood. The chief's house displayed the most skulls, but Paul felt relief when he learned the head man had become a Christian and had no plans to further expand his gruesome collection.

Many children suffered eye problems. Paul learned that at birth a midwife or attendant would wipe the newborn's eyes with a leaf, causing an infection. Life was no easier for the new mother who gave birth tied to a Y-shaped tree trunk—one leg fastened to each limb of the tree. Many children died during childbirth or soon after.

Paul stood on the riverbank almost overcome with the need but thankful that the chief had become a Christian; for when a chief believes, the people follow. "Lord," he prayed, "show me ways to help these people and others like them."

But even as he stood there, deep in his subconscious, a plan had begun to form.

Bridging the cultural gap
Tiny streams bubble down hillsides to begin their journeys to the sea, not knowing that one day they will join others and become a great river. Similarly, men and women, alone but inspired by God, develop plans that will one day complement each other to become a great force in world evangelism. Paul Chang did not know as he stood on the riverside in Kalimantan that Chris Marantika—studying in faraway Dallas, Texas—had developed a master plan for evangelizing Indonesia.[55] Chris would soon return to Indonesia and, on the island of Java south of Kalimantan, establish a church-planting seminary with the goal of planting a church in every village in the country.

Neither could Paul know Anand Chaudhari who, only a few years earlier, had returned to his native India to resume a radio ministry and subsequently devise a plan that eventually resulted in hundreds of new churches across northern India.[56]

Before rising into heaven, Jesus left a final word with his disciples. He said, ". . . you will be my witnesses in Jerusalem, and in all Judea and Samaria, and to the ends of the earth."[57]

The early Christians had done just that. They began at Jerusalem with their own people, then moved on to a neighbouring ethnic group, the Samaritans. From there, they eventually carried the message around the world. When the Romans sacked Jerusalem, it accelerated the process; Christians among the fleeing residents carried the gospel message with them.

So if the Jewish dispersion had become God's tool for spreading the Word, could God also use the Chinese dispersion? Over the centuries Chinese traders had established centres of Chinese culture beyond the traditional borders of their land. When the Communist forces overran China following the Second World War, millions of Chinese fled their homeland and settled in Indo-China and other countries in Southeast Asia.

In Kalimantan Chinese evangelists had planted an ethnic Chinese church. That church reached out to its neighbours, the Dayak people. God had built bridges across the cultural gap between the Christian Jews in dispersion and the Samaritans and then on to the rest of the world. Now God was building bridges from Chinese Christians in dispersion to the tribal people and on to that great mountain of people in the rest of the world.

Paul Chang already had a well-developed missionary vision. Now he had an enlarged dream: he would help build those bridges.

Not far away, in Malaysia, James Lai was then studying at Malaysia Christian Training Centre and would soon join Paul in his great vision. James, born into an ethnic Chinese family in Malaysia, worshipped ancestors and idols and knew nothing about the Christian faith until a friend invited him to church at age 13. After receiving Christ and attending a church retreat, he had surrendered his life for service to God.

CHAPTER 9: *A Family on the Move*

Of Himself, Jesus said, "Foxes have holes and birds of the air have nests, but the Son of Man has no place to lay his head."[58]

In Singapore the Changs lived in the recently purchased, multi-use building on Braddell Road—it contained offices for CNEC, space for a church, and an apartment for the field director. Living right at the convergence point of your church, your home life, and your work has both advantages and drawbacks. The convenience of going to work or church without leaving the building hardly balances the disadvantage of living in the proverbial fish bowl or railway station. Even shutting themselves into the apartment didn't stop the encroaching noises.

***

Mark, then ten years old, remembers that time—he recalls it as his first encounter with demon possession. A lady from the church attended a retreat with members of the CNEC staff. On returning from the retreat, she stayed over with others in the guest room in the office just a wall-thickness from the Chang apartment. During the night, she became agitated and asked someone to read the Bible to her, but soon began screaming and cursing. In Mark's words, "She made sounds like a cat on fire—so loud the entire neighbourhood could hear it."

Paul called together a group of church leaders and worship singers who sang, prayed, and read the Bible for most of three nights. Throughout that time the woman continued screaming and crying. Mark remembers, "It was intense. My sister and I slept with our mom. But the screaming was too much to bear; we finally went to stay with some church friends. It was my first encounter with spiritual warfare and it deepened my belief in God. After four days, the demons left her and she was fine."

***

One year after moving to Singapore, the Changs packed their bags and headed for the airport. This time they relocated from Singapore to California so Paul could raise funds to support the ministries in West Kalimantan and northern Thailand. Mark and Ruth, who had separated from friends and school in Hong Kong, now parted from new friends and schools in Singapore and headed for another land and a different culture. "Where," they wondered, "will we live next year?"

"At least," thought Ruth, "we will always be together as a family."

They settled in San Rafael, California. There Paul hit the road alone, picking up a pattern he knew well—travelling thousands of miles, from church to church and conference to conference to challenge Christians to support the growing work of CNEC in Southeast Asia. Meanwhile Nien-chang hit the books. She enrolled in a graduate program at Golden Gate Baptist Theological Seminary. Her mother came from Boston for an extended visit to help with the children.

Ruth recalls that both she and Mark battled with identity problems in San Rafael: "Mom and Dad tried to speak to us in Chinese but we were reluctant participants. We were American—not Chinese. So, my brother and I really lost a lot of our Chinese when we stayed in America for that period of time."

Eggs
While Paul ostensibly lived in California, he spent most of his time on the road doing deputation work or taking tours of pastors and supporters to the field. On each trip he gathered new information, discovered even greater needs, and faced new personal challenges. While those challenges sometimes involved physical danger, they more often concerned personal likes and dislikes, things like food preferences.

More that one missionary entering a tribal area and facing a strange meal has altered the words of an old hymn to say *Where he leads me I will follow, What he feeds me I will swallow.* On one excursion into tribal territory with a group of visitors, the head man offered Paul and friends a delicacy reserved only for important visitors. The food consisted of eggs buried underground for months until they reached a state of rare ripeness.

Paul looked at the delicacy, wondering if he dared refuse to eat. To do so might offend and cut future access into the tribe, but to eat might result in serious health consequences. Then he saw the food move; it boasted a rich colony of maggots. His stomach began to churn. Placing his hand over the offending organ, he said quite truthfully, "I am not feeling well. I had better not eat."

Missionary kids, used to living in Hong Kong and Singapore and transplanted to California, also have bad moments when faced with food choices. The Changs, attending the CNEC family camp in Mount Hermon, sat with Allen Finley at the breakfast table in the big airy dining hall in the conference centre.

A waitress placed a bowl of scrambled eggs on the table. Ruth and Mark screwed up their faces and exchanged glances. They hated eggs. They had acquired that dislike in Hong Kong where eggs from China often arrived at the table spoiled, smelling, and tasting terrible. The children had no intention of eating scrambled eggs and would not have taken any if a kindly adult had not spooned some on their plates. Ruth, taking her cue from Mark, covered the untouched eggs with a table napkin.

After breakfast, the hostess came to clear the plates. She picked up the silverware and napkins and left the eggs exposed for all to see. Ruth glanced at the adults and saw what she interpreted as a look of disapproval on the CNEC president's face and embarrassment on her parents faces.

Nien-chang jumped to the children's defence by saying, "They don't eat eggs much overseas since the eggs there are often spoiled!"

Today Ruth says, "If someone had told me that eggs were different in America, I would have tried them. But, the unpleasant memories of rotten eggs made me vow not to eat them. Living cross-culturally often instills faulty negative beliefs about things. Today, I still don't eat scrambled eggs!"

Cannibals, witch doctors, and new ministries

In 1976 as part of Paul's deputation work he took to the West
Kalimantan field a group consisting of Harold Stevens,[59] and six
pastors from the US. They travelled by bus from Pontianak to
Empaong, a Dayak village. Harold had played football as a
young man and still had the physique to go with it. An elderly
Dayak man, obviously impressed with Harold's size, stepped up
to him, pushed a finger into his chest, and said, "Thirty years
ago we ate the last white man like you who came to visit us."

On another trip to the area, Paul and a group of visitors
stayed in a local house. In the morning a group of Dayak people
stood nearby clapping. Paul and company stepped outside to see
what had provoked the applause. One member of the tribal
group explained. "The witch doctor put a curse on you, telling
us you would not come out alive. We came to see if that had
happened, but when we saw movement in the house, we realized
you were alive and we began clapping."

Paul explains the significance of that event. "The Dayaks
seemed like a simple people, but we learned that you must not
disappoint them. The witch doctor had disappointed them and
consequently lost credibility."

It soon became apparent that the church behind the mud
hole could not stay in that location much longer: it continued to
grow; urbanization began creeping in; and they felt pressure
from a growing Catholic church. They found land, bought it,
and built a church that would seat three to four hundred people.

The Dayak's lacked trained workers, so they sent trainees to
Chris Marantika's new school—the Evangelical Theological
Seminary of Indonesia (ETSI) in Yogyakarta, Indonesia, and to
other schools. Unfortunately, the prospective workers rarely
returned, opting to work in some other field. In later years, they
found the answer—ETSI established a mini seminary in West
Kalimantan.

Back to Singapore

In May of 1977 Nien-chang completed a Master of Religious
Education degree. In June the four Changs prepared to return to

Singapore—Paul had accepted the appointment as director of the Southeast Asia field. Now they could return to Singapore and settle down as a family and adopt a more conventional home life.

However, missionaries rarely follow a conventional lifestyle. Within a few years the Chang children had changed countries four times: from the United States to Hong Kong; to Singapore; return to the States; back to Singapore. As the countries changed, so did the languages: English, Cantonese and Mandarin. They switched houses and schools even more often.

Before they left San Rafael, Paul and Nien-chang realized that they needed to keep the children occupied as they prepared for the move and enrolled Mark and Ruth in summer school. Ruth took gymnastics and thoroughly enjoyed herself; she had made good friends during the time in San Rafael and bubbled with excitement when she found three of them at the school: Nikki, Alexander, and Alice. That time seemed all too short. Although the experiences of summer school live in memory, Ruth has blanked-out most of the sad times. Try though she may, she cannot remember them packing up their stuff. She doesn't clearly recall her parents dealing with the sadness and grief of leaving—somehow it was just another move, something they did in the service of the Lord.

Ruth does have one picture etched deeply into her memory. On the last day of summer school, just before they left for Singapore, her mother took her to the apartment complex where Alice lived. They drove in a station wagon loaded with their belongings. Together, Nien-chang and Ruth dragged her bicycle from the rear of the vehicle and gave it to Alice. That memory, like a short video clip, ends with Ruth, tears streaming down her face, waving good by to Alice who stood at the curb with the precious bicycle—the blue bike with the silver handlebars.

Ruth snuggled up to her mother. She might lose her bicycle, but wherever they went, they went as a family.

Ruth arrived in Singapore, but things didn't get any easier for a youngster now thoroughly confused about her identity. The Changs moved into the residence of the former field director located in an area of Singapore where many foreigners made their homes. Mark and Ruth attended the local public school, but made friends among the kids they met in the neighbourhood, many of whom attended the American school. On sunny days they played baseball on the streets or on rainy days walked in the open drains filled with rain water.

One day two Caucasian girls arrived at the Chang's gate and invited Ruth to play. They must have considered her unique—a Chinese girl who attended the local school but spoke perfect English with an American accent. To identify with them Ruth said, "I'm an American."

"You are not! You're Singaporean or Chinese," they responded.

"Am not. I'm American."

"You're lying. You're not American."

"Am too!"

"Are not!"

The shouting match continued for a few more rounds before Ruth said. "I'm American and I can prove it. I'll get my passport."

She raced into the house; her passport would identify her as the authentic thing—a real American. "Mom! Where's my passport? I need my passport! Now."

Like most parents, Nien-chang had previously dealt with strange requests from her children and asked the appropriate question, "Why do you need it?"

"I need it Mom. I need it now . . . I . . . I just need it!" Ruth blubbered, but couldn't put the urgent need into the proper words.

Nien-chang shook her head. "No Ruth. A passport is a valuable document. You cannot have it."

Ruth ran outside but found the girls had gone. In despair she banged her head on the metal gate. Her brain seemed to have become waterlogged with her own tears. She couldn't think straight, "I can't even prove who I am. Lord, who am I anyway?"

Ruth's identity problems on the playground amounted to little when compared with her struggles in school. She attended classes where the majority of her classmates looked Chinese and spoke and read the Mandarin dialect of Chinese. Those students who had difficulties in any subject had tutors, but the Chang family could not afford a tutor. Nien-chang did her best to fill that role.

The struggles continued for the next three years, but her memories become much clearer and more painful when she recalls the seventh grade: "I was a very good student. I worked hard but no amount of working made me feel comfortable in Chinese class. When Teacher Wang called me to read aloud, I would cringe inside. My palms would get sweaty as I stumbled through the words on the page. My sympathetic friend sitting behind me would whisper the words I couldn't read. It was such a hopeless feeling, that I think the teacher even gave up asking me questions or making me read."

One day when a substitute teacher called on Ruth to read, the class cried out in unison, "No Teacher! She can't read, Don't ask her."

Ruth remembers the hurt of that day and so many like it. "I looked like everyone else, but inside I was not all Chinese, especially not Singaporean Chinese. My dad and mom said, 'It"s okay'—just do the best and trust. I trusted but I felt terrible about my Chinese. I felt stupid for struggling so much. Educators in Singapore don't grade you for trying; they grade you for excellence."

***

Mark responds differently when he remembers his missionary-kid experiences. Does he do so as the older child? As a boy? Or because he has a very different personality? Whatever the reason, he says of those times: "I moved often from country to country during my middle school years. In fact, we moved almost every year to a different house during our five-year stay in Singapore (before I left for Faith Academy in the Philippines). This was because as foreigners, we could not buy a house in Singapore so we rented. After my parents became permanent residents years later, they bought a flat.

"I don't remember complaining about moving. It felt natural as a missionary family. In fact, I was proud to be an MK. Another great thing about being an MK—I had close friends from many countries. So I have a greater understanding and appreciation of cultures and customs.

"During those years in Hong Kong and Singapore, my dad would keep us children content with different pets. I had a huge tortoise in a flat in Hong Kong (until it disappeared; I think some neighbours cooked it). I also had a baby chick. In Singapore, we had dogs—Dad smuggled one from Malaysia during one of his many trips to the churches. Rabbits, white mice, the usual gold fish, chickens—we got eggs regularly and eventually fresh chicken meat when the rooster's crowing got to the neighbours."

***

By 1977 the West Kalimantan field had started a Sponsor-a-Child program, a high school in Empaong, and an orphanage and student centre. They quickly expanded from ministering to Chinese and Dayaks, including other tribes and Javanese settlers sent there by the Indonesian government. Chinese traders continued making contact with other tribes and some Chinese people even intermarried with the Dayaks. The Chinese community had become a bridge to the tribes—the Acts 1:8 model had begun to work.

In the midst of opening new fields and strengthening existing programs, Paul did not neglect his music ministry. In late 1977, with help from Hannah Koh and Tom Lim from Hong Kong, he completed the hymnbook, *Hymns of Praise*. CNEC Singapore published it in 1978. Printed in both English and Chinese, the book has found acceptance in Chinese communities in many countries.[60]

CHAPTER 10: *Thailand and David Soo*

*"How beautiful on the mountains are the feet of those who
bring good news, who proclaim peace, who bring
good tidings, who proclaim salvation . . ."*[61]

In his first year as interim field director, Paul also visited
Thailand, another field that would become a key part of his
ministry.

The Kingdom of Thailand—a constitutional monarchy formerly known as Siam—has the distinction of being the only
Southeast Asian nation who have never come under the rule of
a Western power. Thailand has a population 95 per cent
Buddhist, but does not place extreme restrictions on Christians,
although missionaries working in that land find it best to keep a
low profile. Paul describes appropriate evangelism methods as,
"the creative-access or holistic-gospel approach."

When Chinese workers affiliated with CNEC first targeted
Thailand in the 1950s, they concentrated on the communities in
northern Thailand settled by Chinese refugees. These settlers
lived in remote villages located in the lowest extremities of the
Himalayan foothills near the border of China and the upper
reaches of the Mekong River.

Here in this fabled land, Paul met David Soo[62]—a man
whose work touched thousands of lives. David had established a
church and living quarters for his family at Hwei Hai, a village
about 40 kilometres north of Chiangrai on the edge of the infamous Golden Triangle. From this area he trekked through the
lush mountains and valleys in search of villages receptive to the
gospel. Typically, he began by preaching to the Chinese communities, then challenging them to reach out to the tribal
groups. Paul Chang and David Soo quickly formed a powerful
bond—they each had exactly the same vision.

David Soo never looked for the easy way or for light
assignments. He targeted the corner of the Golden Triangle that
protruded into northern Thailand. He saw this area as his personal acreage in God's vineyard—an area world famous as the

centre of opium production, controlled by opium warlords, and outside the reach of the central government.

On one occasion, carrying a makeshift backpack—simply a cloth bag—he walked six hours to the heart of the Golden Triangle. Arriving at the village of Hwei Ph'ng he found the chief's daughter in a disturbed state. When he gave her a gospel tract, she became even more agitated, even terrified. He concluded a demon had taken possession of her and offered to pray for her. The chief expressed his willingness, in fact he had reached the end of his rope and had planned to offer his daughter as a sacrifice. He had also dedicated a plot of land for building a temple. David prayed and the demon fled. The grateful chief arranged for the building of a church instead of a temple—they completed it in three days.

On one visit David took Paul to the village. He didn't ask him to walk but hired a man with a World War II Jeep. The owner had modified the vehicle for rough-country travel by equipping it with oversize wheels. He also had removed the gas tank, replacing it with a plastic tank mounted inside the vehicle—a hose connected the makeshift tank directly to the engine. On some inclines, he drove a short distance and asked the passengers to jump out and block the wheels. He repeated the procedure many times, climbing the inclines in fits and starts. When they arrived, Paul slept in a grass hut with the sounds of chickens and animals continuing all night.

David Soo had successfully opened his corner of Thailand's Golden Triangle to the gospel.

***

From inside Hwei Hai Holy Grace Church, David could clearly hear the whine of a distant motorcycle—bamboo shutters don't offer much protection from outside noise. He had just met with the chief of the village of Hwei Ph'ng, his old friend Yang Pang, who had come to request more help with the school in his village.

David sat musing on the great successes in Hwei Ph'ng: the

number of new believers; the recently completed church building; the Grace Light School with 250 students; the effective Sponsor-a-Child ministry; and his temporary dwelling where he stayed when he walked there to minister on most weekends. "What a victory for the Lord!" he said aloud.

The sound of the motorcycle, now nearby, again caught his attention. It slowed as it passed the church, its two-cycle engine emitting an uneven sputter. Then three sharp explosions overcame the sound of the machine. "Backfire," thought David, fully familiar with the eccentricities of small motorbikes.

The engine, now screaming at full power and accompanied by the noise of a spinning rubber tire, sped through the echo of the last explosion.

David stiffened as the truth dawned. "Gunfire," he whispered as though a fleeing assassin might hear and come for him.

Regaining his composure, he hurried from the church to see Yang Pang lying motionless on the road. As he ran forward, he noted blood pooling beneath the body. His friend lay dead.

David carried the body to the church, washed him in the baptismal tank, and buried him in the new cemetery across the road.

***

David learned later that the opium warlord had arranged the murder. He stopped short of killing David, but ordered him to relinquish leadership of the Hwei Ph'ng church and to forget any plans to move to the town. Such an order didn't handicap David; it merely broadened his horizons, freeing him to evangelize other villages.

When Paul first visited in 1976, David had already hired a local teacher, started a school, and established a Sponsor-a-Child program. CNEC assisted by building a multi-room school with student dormitories. Some students walked for two months to attend school—one child stayed at the school for six years without ever going home. In a few years the school grew from 50 to 550.

Boonprasert Vijitrakul, an ethnic Chinese with Thai citizenship, had become a Christian at age 15 in the first CNEC church, Truth Church, located in Chiangrai in northern Thailand. His life and ministry would soon become associated with David Soo and eventually Paul Chang.

In 1973 at age 20 while attending a youth camp, Boonprasert felt the call of God and began looking for ways to serve the Lord. In 1978 he attended the Thailand Baptist Theological Seminary. After completing the three-year course he went to Singapore Bible College for a one-year course.[63] He returned to Thailand and joined the pastoral staff of Truth Church and made visits to Chinese and tribal villages in the mountains of northern Thailand. There he got to know David Soo and see him in action. Years later, his wife Boon Har told this story: "Paul really loved David Soo. Years ago when David worked in an isolated village, Paul and Nien-chang decided to visit him, even though the roads were very poor, they were feeling ill at the time, and they had no official reason to go. Nien-chang told me that when they met David, Paul had tears in his eyes—a very rare thing for Paul."

***

Although Paul managed, most of the time, to conceal his emotions from co-workers and present what he thought of as the face of a firm leader, he couldn't always fool his children.

Mark Chang says: "When attending Faith Academy (high school) in the Philippines, my dad came to visit me. He saw my report card—I was not going to show him because I had received an "F" in history. When he left, he cried in the van that took him to the airport. I never talked to him about that, but I think I understand now as a father of three boys."

Entertaining angels unawares?
Over time, travelling into the Golden Triangle became easier. Better roads began to appear—often financed by the local opium warlord. Paul made numerous trips, frequently taking

overseas visitors. Modern small trucks had replaced the ancient Jeep, but the sense of adventure remained.

***

With agonizing creaks and groans, the battered, white Isuzu pickup worked its way through the ruts and washouts of a dirt road in northwestern Thailand. The tiny truck may not have felt pain from each bump and lurch, but Phil Dempster did.[64] Unable to fold his 1.9 metre[65] frame onto one of the bench seats inside the cage covering the back of the tiny vehicle, he opted to stand on the rear bumper and cling to the top of the cage. Three other visitors from America and Australia shared the seats with an assortment of suitcases. Paul Chang had also chosen to ride the bumper with Phil.

From his precarious perch, Phil had a glorious view of the mountainous countryside. It almost made up for the pounding handed out by vehicle and road. When he crouched down to ease his straining muscles, he could look through the rear window of the cab and see Allen Finley beside the diminutive Thai driver named Sompong.

With bursts of nervous energy, Sompong battled steering wheel and gear shift, guiding the truck through washouts that threatened to swallow both vehicle and passengers. Contrasting with the driver, Phil could glance sideways to see Paul, calm, even stoic, swaying in time with the truck's gyrations. He knew Paul felt safe for he had insisted that David Soo hire the driver who had chauffeured him on previous visits to the remote village.

Early that morning, they had passed through a checkpoint, marking the beginning of the tribal area and signalling their exit from territory under government control. A pole lowered across the road stopped traffic. A sign inscribed in several languages said: "Warning! Register here. Beyond this point it is unsafe to travel. Proceed at your own risk."

Soldiers with grim faces and armed with automatic rifles had examined passports and waved them on. At that point, they had entered Southeast Asia's infamous Golden Triangle. Now they travelled through territory dominated by the local opium warlord. Others, neighbouring war barons and roving bandits, challenged for control of the trade using the road, and for domination of the opium fields hidden high in the mountains of this no-man's land that encroached on the territory of Thailand, Laos, Burma, and China.

Phil paid little attention to the area's political problems, focusing instead on the pastoral scenery. As the road swung past a green rice paddy tucked against a mountainside, the tall grass between paddy and road parted. A young man carrying an automatic rifle emerged and waved down the vehicle. Phil felt his hands tighten on the cage and his heart rate increase, as sweat formed on his brow.

While the gunman exchanged the briefest of words with the driver, Phil noticed a shadow of distress cross Paul's face. In a moment the gunman waved them on, but leaped on the rear bumper with Phil and Paul. The gunman spoke briefly to Paul in Mandarin and Phil's tension slowly drained away, although he wondered what their new passenger wanted.

***

Years later Allen Finley remembered that event in September of 1979 with mixed feelings. "Many thoughts raced through my mind, as the man with the gun stepped into the road. I had concern for myself and the others, since Paul Chang and I were the reason they came on this trek! The man's expression did not betray either friendliness or hostility as he approached and boarded the truck. His clothes did not identify him. No one explained who he was or why he boarded our vehicle. After the initial moments of concern, I recall feeling a sense of well-being, somehow this seemed a good thing."

Phil recalled the incident this way, "Happily for me, Paul did not reveal that the local opium warlord had sent his agent to 'protect' us from local bandits as we travelled through the area. We rode on in blissful ignorance. The man stayed with us for about 40 minutes, but as we approached the village, he signalled the truck to slow, jumped off, and ran into the woods."

Another happening etched the incident firmly onto Paul's mind. The following year he retraced his steps to visit David Soo. Before he boarded a different truck than the one he usually hired, he tensed. "Where is Sompong? He always drives me. I trust him."

The new driver shrugged. "Not available," he said, volunteering nothing further, neither smile nor frown.

Beyond the government check point, deep into the mountains, past the rice paddy where the mysterious protector had appeared, Paul found the answer. The burned, rusting body of the white Isuzu lay at the roadside. When the driver noted Paul's anxiety, he said, "All Dead."

Inexplicably, the words of a hymn echoed through Paul's mind: *He could have called ten thousand angels . . .* Last year, had the opium warlord sent them a flesh-and-blood protector? Or had the Lord of Lords dispatched just one angel from his legions to escort them safely through the valley of the shadow of death?

By all means

On his frequent visits to Hwei Hai, Paul taught the school boys to play basketball. The village of Ban Hin Taek, 25 kilometres from Hwei Hai, also had a primary school. In due course they sent a basketball team to challenge the Christian school. Although it seemed a simple school rivalry, it had major implications—the opium warlord, Khun Sa, claimed Ban Hin Taek as his seat of power. He wanted no interference from the Christians in Hwei Hai or from the Chinese preacher and basketball coach who often visited the school. This outsider seemed to have developed a solid following even in neighbouring villages.

At first he stirred up the people to demonstrate against Paul. When that didn't work, he ordered Paul not to visit the town. Eventually, Khun Sa capitulated—he had seen the effectiveness of the Christian workers in improving the lifestyle of the people and invited them to visit Ban Hin Taek. They came and held a Christmas Eve service that drew 1,500 people. Completely overcome, the opium warlord granted them a hilltop location to build a church.

However, another political problem delayed the construction of the church building. Using the hilltop location would put the church on higher ground than the local Buddhist temple and so offend many local people. The Christian workers solved the problem by finding another plot of land at a lower altitude. On completion of the building in 1986, they asked Boonprasert to dedicate it—for him a never-to-be-forgotten experience.

The Thai government forces eventually wrested the towns and villages from the opium warlord, sending him into exile in Myanmar. However, he continued to exercise control over the poppy fields and opium production situated in Thailand's secluded mountain valleys.

As the government assumed authority over the civil administration, it also wanted the schools. Paul immediately saw the advantage of this: the government would assume the operating costs; the people would learn to speak the Thai language; it would open the door for full Thai citizenship for those who had lived as refugees. The local people initially resisted because the schools would lose their Christian character. However, they reached consensus and CNEC turned over all three schools in the Golden Triangle area. Although the authorities placed large statues of Buddha at the gates of the Hwei Ph'ng and Hwei Mok schools and required students to bow to them, they allowed the churches to run their own teaching program before and after regular school hours.

***

In 1987 Boonprasert moved to the tourist capital of northern Thailand, Chiangmai, to plant a church. In this bustling city of about 500,000—then home to two universities and considered Thailand's second city—he found life more complicated, hectic, and busy than Chiangrai and the villages of the north. In June of that same year he married Boon Har.

***

On-the-job training

Many young people came to Paul for counsel as they wrestled
with plans for the future and sought God's will for their lives.
When they seemed serious, Paul would suggest a three-month
missionary assignment in northern Thailand.

Lily Tan, a nurse, agreed to a short-term assignment at
Hwei Ph'ng and found it so challenging she returned for a second term. She happened to be there when the Thai government
forces attacked the opium warlord and stayed on after her
appointed time to help the injured. Following her short-term
experiences, Lily attended Singapore Bible College, married,
and felt God's call to the mission field. She later went to Liberia
to work with Bishop Gus Marwieh who led a CNEC ministry
there.[66]

Six other short-termers, all men, attended the Singapore
Bible College, became full-time workers, and returned to northern Thailand where they became pastors.

CHAPTER 11: *Emotional Roller Coasters*

*George Moore said, "A man travels the world over in
search of what he needs and returns home to find it."*

Although fully involved in ministry to Chinese and tribal people
throughout Asia, Paul could not forget his homeland. During
the mid 1970s he had an opportunity to become involved in a
project that combined ministry to people in China with the
adventure of a cloak-and-dagger operation.

Bibles remained very scarce in China despite the highly
publicized stories of Bible smuggling. Many key Christian leaders did not have a usable copy of the Scriptures, so a group of
Christians in China decided to hand-print their own New
Testament. They could not buy paper, so CNEC under Paul's
direction sent in household appliances—television sets, radios,
and similar items. The clandestine printers traded the appliances
with government officials for paper. They could not buy ink in
China, and could not import it without raising suspicion, so
Paul sent in a supply mixed in with a shipment of paint.

Working by hand with very crude equipment, the printers
produced 29 copies of the precious book—they could do no
more because their wax-paper masters could handle only 29
impressions.

At about the same time Paul arranged to support a pastor in
China who undertook to train 16 workers. For many years a
sum equal to eight hundred US dollars per month supported the
pastor and his trainees.

A visa for Paul Chang
Cracks had begun to appear in the bamboo curtain. In 1979 the
Chinese government issued a visa so Paul could visit China.

***

As the great pistons coaxed the giant drive wheels into motion,
a burst of exhaust steam shattered the evening air, and a rumble

of energy travelled the length of the train bringing each car to life. The night train to Guilin pulled out of the Changsha station. Paul Chang stared out the dust-streaked window with a sense of confusion as the city slipped by. Its monotone factories and warehouses blended with the people in their drab Mao jackets. His memories of China had always shone with full colour, but now the monotony of black and white overwhelmed him. Yet nothing could fully suppress the excitement building up inside; the click-clack of steel wheels on steel rails echoed one incredible thought, "Going home, going home, going home."

For 30 years, ever since fleeing China as a refugee, he had dreamed of this moment, of this journey—a dream always suppressed by feelings of sheer hopelessness.

Now the miraculous had happened. By morning he would be home. By morning he would meet his mother face-to-face.

He wasn't sure who would meet him when the train pulled into Guilin station. He'd written his oldest brother telling of his permit to visit China, but the pressures of the moment left no time for a reply. He knew his eighty-one-year-old mother still lived, even though long periods of time had passed without news and he had feared the worst. During the Cultural Revolution in the late '60s, six years had passed without one word relating to his family.

Paul had booked a one-passenger sleeping compartment in hopes of getting a good night's sleep before meeting his family. The past few days had been full. He'd travelled through Hong Kong to Guangzhou, where he'd unexpectedly met some Christians who promised to distribute the Bibles he'd brought with him. After taking a night train to Changsha, he'd spent the next day looking in vain for signs of the Bible school and church he had attended there many years ago. Yes, tonight he should sleep.

Turning off the light, Paul pulled his heavy coat over his head and settled down on the hard berth. But sleep wouldn't come; it seemed the wheels had once again picked up their click-clack refrain: "Going home, going home, going home."

Paul lay halfway between sleep and wakefulness, his mind

replaying his teenage flight from China, and the terror of clinging to the outside of railway cars. Suddenly the train jerked to a
halt, bringing Paul back to the present. He bolted upright on the
bunk, an inexplicable fear clutching his throat. His memories
had so overpowered him, it took him a moment to rebound back
to the present. Rubbing a spot on the steamed up window, he
saw they had entered a small town—the name on the station,
like so many names in China now—was unfamiliar. In a moment
the lone disembarking passenger disappeared down the platform,
and the train renewed its journey into the night. Paul noted a
faint touch of colour in the east—the new day would soon
dawn. His heart leaped with praise to his heavenly Father, who
was answering his prayer of 30 years.

As he settled back on the bunk, he realized he still had his
arms clutched protectively around his coat—an automatic ges-
ture that had occurred when the train stopped, waking him from
his reverie. Often over the years train rides had done this to him,
causing him to relive that terrible ride out from Changsha to the
safety of Guilin. As the train moved on, Paul settled back to the
hypnotic sounds of the wheels rushing toward home and let his
memories sweep over him once more.

As the train neared Guilin the sun shone brightly. Paul saw
again the breath-taking grandeur of the "pointed" mountains of
the area. Surprisingly the countryside had changed very little in
the 30 years since he'd left; but he knew the people had changed
a great deal. His father had died—Paul knew he would soon
hear the full details of that sad story. Bits and pieces had come
to him over the years, though letter writers from China always
carefully guarded their wording. They left too much to the
imagination.

Paul reviewed what he knew of his father's death. His
brother had written in 1962 that his father had died. There were
rumours that he had been imprisoned and a report attributed to
his father had appeared in a Peking newspaper, entitled,
"Changes in My Thoughts."

Many Christian leaders suffered intensive periods of "re-
education," and though Professor Chang had never renounced

his faith, the report claimed he made this statement: "I will stand with the great mass and obey the leadership of Chairman Mao, root out all anti-revolutionary activities that eternal peace and blessing and happiness may soon materialize in this great and democratic China, so rich in resources."

Paul had heard nothing from or about his family in China during the years of the Cultural Revolution. During that time thousands of Christians faced imprisonment, torture, and death. He would soon learn how other members of his family had fared. They in turn would learn of God's dealing with him over the years. He smiled in anticipation of giving his mother the things he had brought for her: a large-print Chinese Bible and a tape recorder and tapes of his music.

He knew his story would thrill her. She and his father had sent him out to train for Christian service. He had done so and now had many exciting things to share.

The train pulled into Guilin. He jumped onto the platform, wondering if he would recognize his brother in this mass of humanity where everyone dressed the same. He had worried in vain for he recognized a smiling face coming towards him—and then three others who gathered around him! All four of his brothers who still lived in China reached out to hug and greet him with tears flowing unashamedly. He had not even dared hope to meet all of them.

The three who worked in other cities had arranged time off to meet their long-lost brother. Paul quickly caught up on their lives, finding that they all held responsible positions and had earned the respect of their communities. He learned that Bao-wen taught English in one of the country's top schools—the Guilin Middle School.[67] He also served in the Guilin Christian Church where his father had served. Bao-whie worked as a national basketball referee; Bao-an, a medical doctor, headed Hwei-Nam Hospital in a coal-mining and steel-making area of Central China. Bao-en taught metallurgy in a university. All had remained true to the Lord through the long years of persecution.

The five brothers piled into a van that Bao-wen had borrowed from the local hospital where his wife worked. He drove them to the apartment his mother shared with him and his wife.

When they stopped in front of the building, Bao-wen told Paul, "We live on the third floor. Mother can handle the stairway, but at eighty-one she has to do so slowly. She's up there waiting for you." Then he added understandingly, "We'll wait down here while you go up."

As Paul bounded up the stairs with the package containing the big Bible under his arm, 30 years dropped away. He become once again the teenage boy calling out, "Mother, I'm home."

His mother sat waiting for him near the kitchen door. Neither could speak for a long time; they both cried. Paul handed her the Bible and she uttered her first words, a prayer: "Thank you God, you have answered my prayer. God you have preserved my son and put him in ministry, following in his father's footsteps."

Then she asked Paul, "What have you missed? What food do you want?"

Paul had no hesitation in answering. He listed off: "Egg flour and green-pea soup, Chinese dumplings, and steamed buns."

His mother made note; she would make all of those things during the next four days.

When the others joined them, they closed the door, and the whole family prayed to their Heavenly Father. Remembering what a special time he had experienced, he later said, "Those days we had together were precious—we had family prayer and studied the Bible together. We sang many of the old songs that our parents had taught us. My brother played the accordion. We sang duets and read Scriptures. Once my mother took a little piece of paper from her pocket to show me, saying, 'This used to be by my Bible.' It was all she'd had for fifteen years. She told me that the new Bible with big letters was the most precious gift I'd brought for her."

Paul stayed in a hotel, but spent almost every waking moment with his family and others who arrived to greet him. Some of his father's students and friends came and shared their stories. All had suffered persecution; some had undergone torture. They treated Paul like royalty—they thought him special because he had come to see them from the outside, from Singapore and the United States!

During their busy time together Paul and his brothers accepted invitations to two official dinners, one hosted by the city council, the other by the department of education. The officials treated Paul with great courtesy and respect.

When not at official functions or meeting with friends from years gone by, they chatted about old times and caught up with the news of each other's families. Paul left thanking the Lord for His goodness and mercy toward his family and for his mother's good health at the age of eighty-one.

Meanwhile at home

With Paul caught up in one of the most emotional experiences of his life—the return to China and the rediscovery of his family— the next generation of the Chang family soon found themselves at the opposite end of the emotional spectrum. Ruth even wondered if the family had begun to disintegrate.

Mark found himself in real trouble in the Singapore school system. They had directed him into a vocational track following the release of his O-level results. Ruth had a very different view of her brother's scholastic abilities. "I was so mad. My brother was smart. He could take apart things and put them together. When people from America came to train the CNEC staff on computers, he was the one who got it. He was brilliant in my eyes, creative, smart, very resourceful and good with his hands—electronics, making things. The Singapore system really messed him up."

Paul and Nien-chang felt much the same way and, deciding he would do much better in an American-type system, enrolled him at Faith Academy in the Philippines. Somehow they would find the funds. Nien-chang sent him on his way with mixed feelings. She would miss her son, but the closeness of the Philippines to Singapore meant he would come home during the summers. He would have good teachers, and they had Chinese friends living there who would keep an eye on him—and anyway, she still had Ruth with her.

Ruth did not handle the parting as well as her mother. "So, he left. I was alone. Mark and I understood each other. We were both Chinese in colour, but our hearts were multinational. We had been together all over: Hong Kong, America, England, Israel, Australia, countless airports, numerous homes, and not forgetting sitting in a church listening to Dad speak for the fiftieth time. When Mark left, I lost a friend and someone to walk the journey with. He often gave me strength. I thought since he can deal with life, I can too!"

Ruth's credo, "We will always be together," suffered a severe blow.

CHAPTER 12 : *Family Matters*

Confucius said, "When you do things for your parents,
admonish them gently. If you see that they are determined
not to go along, then respect them and do not oppose them;
and do not resent them for the trouble you've taken."

Since the days of the Apostle Paul Christian workers have faced
the challenges of merging family responsibilities with mission
activities.[68] Each family draws from biblical, generational, and
cultural norms when establishing a pattern for raising children.

East and West stand half a world apart when it comes to
child rearing. Pearl S. Buck grew up a westerner in China. She
wrote the following to depict one aspect of family life in China
during her own childhood—about the time that Paul's father,
Chang Hsueh Kung was born.

> Yes, Chinese children were alarmingly spoiled when
> they were small . . . No one stopped tantrums or
> willfulness and a baby was picked up whenever he
> cried . . . Babies ate what they pleased and when they
> pleased, and little children lived a heavenly life. The
> Chinese believed that it was important to allow a child
> to cry his fill and vent all his tempers and humours
> while he was small, for if these were restrained and
> suppressed by force or fright, then anger entered into
> the blood and poisoned the heart, and would surely
> come forth later to make adult trouble. It was a knowl-
> edge as ancient as a thousand years . . . Right or wrong,
> these spoiled children emerged like butterflies from
> cocoons at about the age of seven or eight, amazingly
> adult and sweet tempered and self-disciplined.[69]

***

Ruth Chang has a personal view of her parents child-rearing
skills that better reflects their international backgrounds. She

says, "My parents are Western in many ways. They are not traditional Chinese parents stereotyped to expect their children to be high achievers or to have good professions. They just expected us to do our best and love and follow the Lord. They are however, quite Chinese, when it comes to emotions and the communicating of hard emotions."

Ruth describes two events from her life that clearly reflect Paul and Nien-chang's parenting skills. She says, "One lesson my father and mother taught me is to trust God and His Word and believe in Him because I want to, not because they want me to. They never forced Mark and me to believe what they believed, but they assumed the responsibility to teach us about the Lord. When I was eleven or so, I decided that church was a bore; I didn't want to go. I wanted to stay home and watch the good TV shows on Sunday morning. I could believe in God even if I didn't go to church, I reasoned. I "informed" my mom and dad that I didn't want to go. My parents didn't scold or persuade or give me a lecture. They said I could do what I wanted to do. They made one condition: after a month, I had to ask myself whether or not this was the right thing to do and if it helped me know God. I agreed. It would be fun. I watched TV for four hours straight the first Sunday. The next Sunday, I did the same but halfway through, I got sick of it. On the third Sunday, I went back to church. I knew that television in place of God was meaningless and boring.

"Another time, a year or so later, the TV show *Dallas* was really big in Singapore. My friends all watched it. I wanted to watch it too, but Mom and Dad said it was a bad show, full of impure lifestyles, greed and other bad things. But, I insisted. She said I could watch it for a month, but she wanted me to think about it after one month and decide if the things on TV were good for me. I watched three episodes; it disgusted me. I knew it portrayed bad morals and bad living and I stopped watching it. If they had demanded I stop watching, they would have made me more determined to disobey. They taught me to discern what's good and pleasing to the Lord and what's not."

Paul Chang and his wife Nien-chang

Ruth (nee Chang), Kaitlin, and Peter Lam

Mark Chang, Helina, and the children.

Four generations—family reunion with Nien-chang's mother.

Allen Finley with Paul Chang, 1968

Paul, with Cliff Barrows, as Director of a 5,000-voice choir at the Billy Graham Crusade.

Paul receiving honourary doctorate at Biola University.

Paul with children at orphanage in Myanmar.

Wa Tribe believers gather for worship in Myanmar.

Residents and staff of the New Vision Home, a CNEC drug rehabilitation centre in Myanmar.

Children's ministry in Myanmar.

James Lai and his wife Rachel.

Boonprasert and Boon Har Vijitrakul (fifth and sixth from left) with ministry staff in Thailand.

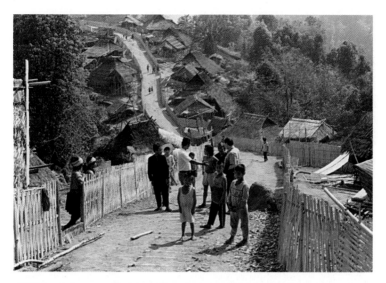

CNEC ministry staff visit village in northern Thailand.

Paul with Akha pastor in northern Thailand.

Chinese congregation near the border with North Korea.

Author Ray Wiseman interviews Paul in Singapore.

***

In 1981 Paul returned for a second four-day visit with his mother. Esther Fan, Lorry Lutz,[70] and Arthur and Betty Gee from the U.S. office of CNEC accompanied him. This time he rented a hotel room for his mother and arranged with the hotel to prepare a banquet for his family and friends—about 40 people in all.

Following the banquet, they returned to the room and had a worship time together. Paul interpreted for Art Gee who preached. Paul then baptized a number of people, including some relatives.[71] One woman, a friend of Paul's mother, came forward and asked for baptism, "I've waited 20 years for this," she said.

In the hotel room, Paul's mother shared the story of his father's arrest and torture. "He starved to death," she said. "His body was little more than a skeleton. When they sent me the message of his death and I went to claim his body, the authorities at the prison described him as 'a good man and a fine Christian.' We buried him in the cemetery within the prison walls."[72]

She paused for a moment, then continued, her voice shaking as Paul clung to every word. "They allowed us to put up a tombstone with the words, 'God's Servant.'"

Another family member picked up the story, "His condemnation brought suffering on others, certainly on Mother, but also on us, his sons. The Communists took away the rights of all of us still living in China."

Another cut in, "Then came the Cultural Revolution and things got worse."

***

The Changs frequently made deputation trips to North America to inform supporters of new developments in the ministry and to keep the needed funds flowing. Often they included family business in their schedule. In 1982, a few months before her

16th birthday, Paul and Nien-chang dropped Ruth off at her maternal grandmother and aunt's house in Boston, Massachusetts.

Ruth describes that event: "I was going to go into 12th grade and live in America. It excited me but I didn't foresee the pain that came from separation from my parents. Though we moved a lot, as a family, we always stayed together—I took that for granted. I did well in Singapore, but the school system gave students very few choices. I was a good student tracked in the pure arts stream studying subjects like literature and history. That streaming gave me no chance to take computers or anything different. So, together with Mom and Dad, we decided that it was better for me to go back to America."

Ruth prepared for her first day at Newton North High School, a few blocks from her aunt's home, as her parents made ready to catch a flight to another city and yet another speaking appointment. The snow fell hard that day. Through the window and through her tears, Ruth watched the flakes fluttering down. Paul didn't say much; he just told her of his pride and love for her.

Ruth remembers: "Before that day, we hadn't talked about how hard it would be to leave each other. We never discussed why life was like this or why couldn't they stay in America for a while. We didn't express in words the sadness of missing each other. I didn't dare ask Dad to stay because I knew he couldn't. There were meetings, schedules to keep. He was on the deputation trail. All the unspoken questions lay dormant in my mind."

As her parents hopped into a car for the airport, Ruth screwed up her courage, walked through the snow to the school and entered—it never snows in Singapore. She looked about and saw something else very different: she saw kids all over—black, white, very tall, very big, and very loud.

She recalls: "I willed myself to stop crying and just make it—just find the classes and go to school. Don't think about the pain of separating from Mom and Dad for a long time. Don't think about missing them. Block out the screaming voice that says, 'Why can't it be different?'"

She found her assigned locker and tried to open the door.

She tried hard but couldn't get it to open. She might have seen a school locker in the movies but never in real life. Finally, after several minutes of pulling and pushing and biting her lips to combat the despair filling her, she turned to a tall brown-haired boy at the next locker.

"Could you open this for me?" she asked, watching his eyebrows arc upward and his mouth drop open.

She just knew he was thinking, "How could anyone not know how to open a locker?"

The locker went *click* and opened. Ruth muttered, "Thanks."

Today she says, "That began my life in America. It ended also for me, the belief that our family would remain together in one place at one time."

Nien-chang also remembers her own hurt at parting from Ruth. "A daughter is closer to her mother. Yes it bothered me to leave her. But she adjusted quickly and did well at school."

Back in Singapore

On Paul's return to Singapore, he threw himself into a new challenge. For years he had not only used music as an adjunct to his personal ministry, he had taught music and worship seminars to help others develop an appropriate philosophy of music in the church. He had developed a close relationship with the Singapore Bible College, worked with their choir, toured with their male quartet, and acted as a board member since 1974.

Now he accepted the opportunity to formalize the music aspect of his personal ministry by establishing the School of Church Music (SCM) at the Singapore Bible College.[73] As founder, faculty member, and dean of SCM, he had an exceptional opportunity to influence future pastors and missionaries from a broad spectrum of Christian denominations. He simply folded the teaching requirements into his otherwise busy schedule.

CHAPTER 13 : *Expanding Ministries*

*Isaiah said, "Enlarge the place of your tent,
stretch your curtains wide, do not hold back;
lengthen your cords, strengthen your stakes,
for you will spread out to the right and to the left . . ."*[74]

Although actually part of Thailand, Hwei Hai stands in a 30-kilometre buffer zone between Thailand and Myanmar.[75] People can easily cross back and forth between countries if they remain within that area. In the late 1970s CNEC had made use of that anomaly by hiring a teacher to run Bible school courses in a church in Thailand within walking distance of Myanmar. The Myanmar students lived in houses in their country, inexpensively rented by CNEC, and daily walked across the bridge spanning the Mekong River into Thailand.

A few years later the Gospel Bible Institute began in Hwei Hai. They arranged for the students to get refugee identity papers so they could remain at the school. This practice continued until Bible institutes became available in Myanmar.

Travelling the Burma Road

The Reverend Yap Un Han, then principal of Singapore Bible College, inspired a new ministry by directing a question to Paul, "Why don't you work in Burma?"

Ready for any new opportunity, Paul asked, "Can I get in?"

"I'll get a contact," came the terse reply.

True to his word, Principal Yap contacted a Myanmar pastor, Rev. Yan Ta Ann who ministered in Lashio in Shan State. He not only agreed to meet with Paul in Chiangmai, Thailand, but walked all the way, over five hundred kilometres, from Lashio in Shan State. The two met for only a half day then returned to their respective home bases. Growing out of that meeting of minds and with assistance from CNEC, Rev. Yan established the Northern Burma Bible Institute and started a Sponsor-a-Child program. He built the school buildings on property behind the church.

A local man, Mr. Cha Tan Yone, who operated a successful business dealing in semi-precious stones became involved in the work from the beginning. By transferring funds through his business, Cha saved much money for the fledgling organization.

In 1982 Xin Min Lu, working closely with Rev. Yan and business man Cha and motivated by the illiteracy of the people and a desire to evangelize, established the Holy Light School in Lashio. He began it as a primary school and soon expanded it to include junior high and high school.

In 1987 Paul visited Shan State, taking a train from Yangon (formerly Rangoon) to Mandalay then travelling northeast by taxi from Mandalay to Lashio. The taxi followed for about 250 kilometres a feeder route to the old Burma Road of World War II fame.

The original Burma road had existed as a trail when spice and tea caravans made their torturous way westward out of China. Kublai Khan's Mongolian warriors had stormed down it from China to conquer Burma after a colossal battle with the army of the King of Burma, then called Mian. Marco Polo travelled up from Mandalay and crossed into China on his fabulous travels in Asia during the 13th century.

After the Sino-Japanese War broke out, the Burmese government built roads to connect their Irrawaddy River ports with the railhead of Lashio and the launching point of the road into China. The road became China's lifeline as overseas workers came in to transport needed military supplies from Burma to China. When the Japanese seized the ports of Burma during World War II, the road lost its importance.

Paul thought about that history as the taxi bounced along a road severely neglected since its heyday. But even in its deplorable condition, it would now have a higher calling as it became a feeder route to CNEC missionaries working in the Lashio area. The dirt road wound across the plain outside Mandalay, then climbed into the foothills where the taxi often struggled along in low gear, navigating steep inclines and hairpin turns, often dipping down into valleys and crossing bridges, relics of a bygone era.

As he bounced along, Paul thought about Burma and the cultural and historic challenges to Christian work there. Since becoming independent and changing the name to Myanmar, the regulations governing missionaries had tightened. The devout Buddhist country tolerated Christianity, but did not allow outsiders to preach. Foreign missionaries had left; the government had nationalized all schools including universities. Every morning devout Buddhists visit the temples and pagodas that dot the countryside. The country's wealth seems to flow into the temples—all that isn't sucked up by a dictatorial government or local opium warlord. Everywhere he looked, Paul saw Buddhist temples and monks and nuns, often only children. Burmese culture dictates that people must feed the monks and nuns; so many people who can't find work join their ranks, effectively burdening those who do work.

After a gruelling ten- to twelve-hour trip Paul reached Lashio. By now CNEC had 30 workers in the area and had opened ten schools. While there he learned something that would eventually change the whole character of the Lashio outreach. Mr. Cha Tan Yone—expert in jade, successful businessman trading in semi-precious stones—wanted to join CNEC as a full-time worker.

At Paul's suggestion, Cha enrolled at Singapore Bible College. While there he met Susan Chang, a student from Hwei Hai, Thailand. They married in Thailand and returned to Lashio to work with Rev. Yan.

In the early 1990s, Paul arranged for Yan to visit Singapore. There he met a wealthy Korean who offered to cover all his financial needs. Soon tensions grew between Yan and the Singapore office over the distribution of funds. Nevertheless, CNEC raised $20,000 to purchase an ex-missionary property for the ministry in Maymyo, but soon after taking possession, Yan withdrew. This left only two key workers who stayed with CNEC: Cha Tan Yone and Xian Yun, the principal of Holy Light School. The ministry in Shan State had temporarily collapsed.

The breakaway work under Yan soon began to disintegrate; the Korean withdrew his support. But under Cha's leadership

CNEC simply started over, and soon surpassed its earlier successes. Within a few years Cha and a group of new workers established eight orphanages and eleven schools. The Holy Light School flourished as Xian Yun built up a good faculty. Its reputation for quality education earned it recognition from the governments of China and Taiwan—though, strangely, not from the educational authorities in Myanmar where anything Christian remains suspect.

In 1985 on a visit to the Philippines, Paul met Kuang Nawni, a woman from Myanmar. She had gone to the Philippines on a study leave to better prepare herself for ministry with her husband, Rev. Phun Duma, an evangelist in Chin State. By 1987 CNEC had begun to work with them, supplying 19 bicycles for evangelists, and funding three pastors to study at Singapore Bible College. They returned to train other local people. The work soon developed to include supported national workers, a Sponsor-a-Child program, and the Bethel Children's Home located in the Yangon area.

Malaysia
Missiologists see the Malays as one of the most unreached people groups in the world. Missionaries entered Malaysia over one hundred years ago, but ministry, mostly among tribal groups, moved slowly. In the late '60s and early '70s, the country began denying missionaries visas to return or enter. Up until then, nationals had accepted little responsibility in reaching their own people—until CNEC Singapore became involved in church-planting ministry. Because of the dominant Islamic population, the law of the land obstructs Christian witness to Muslims. However, it does not stop evangelizing Malaysians of other ethnic and religious backgrounds, so they started among Chinese communities and soon spread out to reach neighbouring tribal groups.

James Lai, after finishing his third year of study at Malaysia Christian Training Centre, joined CNEC and began serving as a church planter. Four years later after successfully planting a church, he moved on to a city church to assume pastoral duties. Over the years, James married, had two children, became an

ordained minister, earned a Master of Divinity degree from
Singapore Bible College, and established the Partners Training
Centre (PTC). PTC is a mobile training program that equips
regional pastors and Christian workers in Malaysia.

In James Lai, Paul Chang had another keen associate to
strengthen the bridges from the Chinese communities to tribal
groups and to Malaysians. In 1995 James became director of the
CNEC Malaysian field.

Christianity re-emerges in China
Since his trips back to China to visit his mother and family,
Paul and others working with CNEC regularly return to China to
assist existing ministries and to establish new outreach works.
Chuck Bennett[76] and a group from CNEC visited China in 1994.
Chuck's description of that event clearly describes the changes
that had occurred in China during the years since Paul's first
visit in 1979.

***

Pop! Pop! Pop-pop-pop-pop-pop-pop-pop-pop!
Minute after minute the explosions kept going—thousands
of them—as two men fed a long belt of firecrackers over the
edge of the roof. Smoke from the machine-gun-like explosions
obscured the building.

We had gone there to "Red Bridge Village" in southern
China to celebrate the completion of a new church building.
And what a celebration it was! Firecrackers and singing and
speeches, plus a sermon. And mountains of food. Our govern-
ment-assigned chaperon from the Bureau of Religious Affairs—
who had to pledge he had no religion in order to get his job—
also gave a speech. I chose my words carefully during my brief
remarks, congratulating them for being part of the largest,
fastest-growing family on earth—the family of Christians.

The guest preacher from another part of China gave a clear
gospel message, then with a shy smile pointed to the government
official sitting next to me. "How many of you will promise to

pray for this man?" he asked the audience. Every hand in the church shot up. "See! Your life is going to change," he teased the government man whose face flushed beet red with embarrassment.

In 1984 there had been only one Christian in Red Bridge Village. She was a young woman from another area who had married a local man and soon won him to Christ. Four years later there were 30 believers in the village. When we visited in 1994, there were 300. And the growth continues. In fact, the number of believers in that local district—or county—grew from 900 to 10,000 during those same ten years.

The woman's first convert, her husband, received training through Partners International and is now the local pastor. However, I came away with the impression that the wife is really the behind-the-scenes leader of the community.

The speed with which people are turning to Christ in China today boggles the mind. When the Communists took control in 1949—a hundred years after missionaries began work in China—there were less than a million Protestant Christians in all of China, plus about three million Catholics. Today there are almost certainly more than 50 million believers. Some people think there may be 100 million. Outsiders like me are only allowed to visit government registered churches such as the one in Red Bridge Village. However, 80 or 90 percent of all churches in China are unregistered, meeting more or less secretly in homes. In some areas local authorities tolerate them. In other areas they are still pursued and persecuted, forced to meet in total secrecy.

Amazingly, God allowed communism to break the hold of the traditional religions and created a deep hunger for meaning in life—a sort of spiritual vacuum that prepared the way for this explosion of church growth.

Before the Communists came to power, each region of China had its own district dialect, virtually unintelligible to others, and only a small percentage of the people could read and write. Mao Zedong imposed Mandarin as the standard language throughout the country and simplified the complex Chinese pictograph writing. Now most people in China understand Mandarin and are able to read and write. This means they are now able to read the scriptures, making it far easier to evangelize and train local leaders than it ever was before.

Furthermore, about 30 years ago the infamous Red Guard movement scattered Chinese Christians all over the country. Like the early believers described in *The Acts of the Apostles*, everywhere they went they talked about Jesus.

Virtually all schools in China were closed for several years during the time of the Red Guards. The generation that missed out on schooling is now in its thirties and forties. Desperate to make up for what they missed, they are some of the most highly motivated students in the world.

This frantic search for learning makes an entire generation more open to the gospel message, but equally open to other religions. Cults and sects abound. One pseudo-Christian sect blanketed the cities with millions of leaflets, urging the people to oppose the government and claiming their leader is Jesus returned to earth. Not surprisingly, the government then cracked down on all Christians.

Tens of thousands of house churches are led by men and women in their twenties. Entire "networks" (quasi-denominations), made up of several thousand house churches have not a single seminary-trained pastor.

These Chinese believers already know how to evangelize effectively. Their great need is for appropriate on-the-job training in Bible and leadership for thousands of local church lay leaders. But it must be on their terms. They insist that training must be appropriate to their culture and their present political situation. Translations of training materials from the West—or even from Taiwan—are rarely effective. They simply don't fit the reality of life inside China today. So the house church leaders in China are now producing most of their own training materials.

It seems like it was only yesterday when I, like most Christians in the West, pretty much gave up on China. We thought a hundred years of missionary work and sacrifice had been lost—-that Christianity had all but disappeared inside the hermetically sealed land of Mao's Little Red Book, Red Guards and "Great Leap Forward." The situation seemed so helpless that most of us even stopped praying for China.

Who could have believed that only 20 years later China would be experiencing the most rapid numerical growth of the Christian faith of any nation in history? But that's what happened.

How like God to cause even the wrath of arrogant men like Mao Zedong to praise him.[77]

***

The following year Paul again returned to China. He said: "I had an opportunity to return to China in September. In the hotel where I stayed, I baptized eight believers—they willingly requested it, having believed with their hearts and confessed with their mouths that Jesus is their only saviour. One of them is a doctor. When I visited the hospital I found six staff members who were Christians, but they have no one to nurture them in their Christian faith. They also need Christian books to help them grow spiritually."[78]

Consequently, Paul devised a plan to supply Bibles to churches in one city during his next visit to China. He took in a group of CNEC supporters, asking each traveller to pack a few Bibles into his or her luggage. If the customs agents confiscated them, they would accept that as of the Lord.

Once checked into their hotel rooms, the visitors would deliver their Bibles to Paul's room. Paul had contacted church leaders in the target city, asking them to pick up the Bibles at his room. The plan called for the local Christians to arrive at Paul's room at specified intervals and carry away a few Bibles each, thus avoid attracting attention.

The travellers happily joined the plan and passed through customs unchallenged. But things went astray on the way from the airport to the hotel. The Chinese Tourist group handling the arrangements dropped Paul and company at a different hotel than originally planned. The visitors all dropped off their Bibles at Paul's room. But the Christian couriers not knowing Paul's whereabouts did not arrive to pick them up.

Paul sat in his room, stared at the pile of Bibles and asked, "Lord, what do I do now?"

He did not know how to contact the pastor with whom he had made the arrangements. He knew that eventually someone, a service person or maid, would come to the room and discover the Bibles and, most likely, report him to the authorities. An unsympathetic official might frown on his importing of Bibles and revoke his privilege to visit China.

Fortunately, the intended recipients realized what had happened, tracked down Paul and the group, and began appearing at the hotel room. Paul breathed easier when the last of the books disappeared.

"Not again," he sighed.

The year 1996 found him back in China. This time to visit a training centre in central China and officiate at a wedding. In the following paragraphs, Paul tells the story. Note that he carefully avoids naming individuals or locations—the degree of freedom in China often depends on the tolerance of local authorities. Confidentiality in reporting Christian activities in China serves a double purpose—it protects local Christians and the government officials who might wink on events that their superiors might disapprove.

***

The Lord's foot soldiers: The wheels of their bicycle kept a steady spin as two young women shared a ride on the unpaved, bumpy roads of central China. It would take them about eight hours to get to the training centre. Sweat mingled with dirt dripped from their tired but excited faces. They were to attend a one-week pastors' training program aimed to equip them to serve the Lord in their own villages.

As I looked out into the audience of 30-some pastors, I saw men and women who, like the two young women, had travelled long distances to come and learn more about the Scriptures in order to teach others about Jesus. Those running the program had assigned me to teach an Old Testament Survey class, conduct a class on hymn singing and lead revival meetings. These classes went from 7:30 a.m. to 9:00 p.m.

Though the days were very long, the students at the training program greatly moved and encouraged me. As I interacted with them, I sensed their eagerness to learn and their thirst for greater understanding of God's Word. Many of them had no previous Bible training; however, they showed great spiritual leadership and felt a tremendous responsibility to train Christian brothers and sisters. Their day-to-day tasks included the encouragement of the body of Christ through persecution, the defense of their faith from being polluted by cults and heresy, and the nurturing of brothers and sisters in their walk with Christ.

As I left the training centre after a week of teaching, seated on a farm tractor, I felt an even greater admiration for my fellow servants of Christ. They were pressing onward, undaunted, with the gospel of peace.

A Christian village wedding: The delighted onlookers listened to the Christian vows as bride and groom openly expressed their love for each other and promised to stay true to the commitment they made to God and each other. It was the first wedding of its kind—where God was glorified openly and the tenets of a Christian wedding explained.

I officiated at this wedding in a farming community because the bride and groom desired to share Christ and His message through their wedding. As I spoke to the couple about the Lord's commands regarding marriage, I marvelled at the chance that God gave me to present Him to all those present.

This wedding ceremony was the first of a Christian marriage. Through this wedding, the participants worshipped God and lifted up his name. As I blessed this newly married couple, I prayed that the people themselves and the authorities would allow many more like it to take place.[79]

***

In 1997 Paul celebrated 50 years since fleeing China by returning to his birthplace. There he alternately experienced both sadness and jubilation. As he walked the area where the seminary had stood, sadness gripped him. He found that most of the old buildings had vanished. He mourned for the ministries that had been such an important part of his father's life. He found virtually no trace of the seminary, the orphanage, the hospital, or the leprosarium. His eyes misted over as he wondered if any people in the city would remember the name Chang Hsueh Kung. He also wondered how many would remember the name that his father had so diligently preached—Jesus Christ.

He should not have concerned himself with the last question. His heart flooded with gladness when he found the city had one hundred, twenty churches, most of them meeting in homes. He experienced a joyful time of worship in one church with three hundred members. He met hundreds of Christians hungry for God's Word and the fellowship of other Christians. During one week he taught intensive Bible classes to a few key leaders. He travelled to villages, some he had last visited as a boy, where he met Christians, held meetings, and trained choirs and conducted workshops.

When Paul returned home he immediately sent off a letter to supporters, listing the things Christians in other lands could do for their fellow believers in China. He said: pray; supply Christian literature; provide Sunday school teaching tools; send qualified instructors to teach the teachers in China.

CHAPTER 14 : *The Holistic Gospel*

Proverbs 22:9 says, "A generous man will himself be blessed, for he shares himself with the poor."

Paul carried a burden unseen by human eyes—a weight he had borne since those early days when he tagged along at his father's side on preaching tours through the Shandong countryside. He had watched his father break a journey to help bury the dead or to aid an indigent peasant. He knew his father had built a mill to help the farmers feed the multitude, maintained an orphanage to house abandoned children, operated a leper colony to care for the sick, and ran a school to rescue the population from ignorance. He had seen his father give up his home so refugees would have shelter. Indeed, his father had risked his life by defying the Japanese Imperial Army to protect refugees, lepers, and orphans.

Paul bore his father's vision: to touch the lives of people where they lived, to help them overcome their social and physical problems. For surely Jesus had said, "I tell you the truth, whatever you did for one of the least of these brothers of mine, you did for me."

By responding to Jesus' words and following his father's example, Paul realized he could relieve suffering and at the same time prepare minds and hearts to receive the gospel message. Out of this thinking Paul developed what he calls "Two Tracks." This ministry philosophy has two aspects, running parallel like railway tracks, one aspect relates to physical and social needs, the other to spiritual needs. He realizes that, like a railway train, his ministry would derail if it tried to run with only one track.

Paul describes his Two-Track or holistic ministry this way:

> The holistic gospel is a combination of evangelism, discipleship, and life-impacting ministry. It is just like the two tracks of the train that cannot be separated. Men need salvation as well as everyday living needs. How

can a church apply faith (God's love) in everyday living? Many a time we do this through life-impacting ministry. The Bible teaches that the greatest commandment is to love one another (John 13:34).

CNEC/PI emphasises the equipping of national workers as we believe that the ministry will ultimately be handed over to them. Thus, setting up Bible colleges and discipleship training centres becomes our priority. . . . Our desire is to model after Jesus Christ's discipleship.

At the same time, we set up orphanages, schools, drug rehabilitation centres, student centres, provide life-skills training like agriculture, medical services and micro-enterprises to touch lives. This helps to testify to Christ's love for all men. With these two types of ministries, the "Gospel Train" will be able to reach out to people without obstruction. The holistic ministry is able to testify to God's power and at the same time equip lives to serve the Lord.[80]

Throughout the '80s and '90s CNEC orphanages proliferated in the Southeast Asian field. Financed by the Sponsor-a-Child program, they soon sheltered hundreds of children, guaranteeing them safety, good nutrition, education, and an opportunity to respond to the Christian message. David Soo early saw the need and began building children's shelters in Thailand; in Myanmar Rev. Cha enthusiastically picked up the challenge and made orphanages a key part of his work.

Myanmar orphanages deserve special mention. Although called orphanages, most of the children who live in the homes have parents who abandoned them or gave them away. Extreme poverty often prompts parents to sell their children. Without intervention or assistance by CNEC workers, many would experience some form of bondage. Slave traders buy girls and spirit them to Thailand where they serve as prostitutes in the red-light district of Bangkok—an area notorious for child prostitution. Sometimes they simply steal the girls—even the families of Christian workers can get caught in the evil net.

***

Martha[81] heard a car approaching around the far bend and stepped off the road to let it pass safely. She watched with disinterest as a battered pickup with a canopy covering the truck bed bumped toward her along the road. She tensed and stepped back as it stopped opposite her. When the driver jumped down from the cab, Martha took another step backward—Mother had warned her that slavers had picked up children along these roads.

"Is this the road to Tachilek?" the driver asked.

Martha hesitated. Everyone knew this road led to Tachilek. "Yes—," she answered.

At that moment a woman emerged from the truck and flashed a big smile. "Martha, its me. How are you and your mother? Is she still pastor of the CNEC Church? I haven't seen her for ages."

The tension left Martha and she approached the woman. "Hello Cousin! Mother and I are fine. How are you? And why are you lost? Surely you know this road leads to Tachilek?"

Before the conversation progressed further, the driver stepped behind her, catching her by the arm. She opened her mouth to scream, but before she could make a sound, she felt a smelly, oily rag clamped over her mouth. The attacker pinned her upper arms and clamped the rag even tighter over her mouth and nose. She fought furiously, kicking back at him, but without effect. Through a blur of tears she saw her cousin smiling and thought, "She's not going to help me!"

Her head began swimming and the energy drained from her body. The two of them carried her, now barely resisting, and tossed her into the back of the truck. "She's a real live little devil, this one," the driver said. "Tie her up."

Martha felt her energy ebbing; she could fight no more. Before slipping into a black hole, she heard the voice of the driver again, "We got us a pretty little one this time. She'll bring plenty of baht when we get her to Bangkok."

Martha awoke to the shaking and bouncing of a rough road. She lay on her back, hands tied in front, feet strapped together, and with a tape gagging her mouth. As she surfaced from mental fuzziness she remembered what had happened. She could see moonlight filtering through the dirt on the windows of the canopy that covered the back of the vehicle. She thrashed about trying to get free, but to no avail. Then she realized someone else lay beside her. In the dim light she could make out another girl about her age, also tied and gagged. She bumped her body against the other but got no response.

The truck stopped. Martha could hear men talking and moving about outside. The girl beside her moved. After about ten minutes, the tailgate swung open and the driver leaned in. "All right my little beauties, time for a rest stop."

He grabbed Martha's foot and dragged her out, catching her before she fell to the ground. He stood her up and ripped the tape from her mouth. "Don't bother to yell. No one will hear you. I'll untie your feet now so you can relieve yourself. Then you can have something to eat."

Martha stumbled toward a thicket thinking, "This is too late. I soaked myself when I was drugged."

She stood out of sight of the men who seemed to be making camp. A second man had taken the place of the woman, her cousin. She heard the crackle of a camp fire and the voice of the driver, "We'll stay here for two or three hours then cross into Thailand. We have to meet the van at three o'clock."

The mention of Thailand terrified Martha. She had heard of the brothels of Bangkok where stolen and enslaved children serve the perverted wishes of tourists from Japan and America. She had just made it to the road out of sight of the truck and began to run when she heard the second man yell, "Where is that girl? Find her!"

Martha sped along the dirt road, hampered by a lost shoe and tied hands. The man caught her and dragged her back. She nearly collapsed from the sting of a stick across her back. "Don't hit her, the driver yelled. They don't want damaged merchandise."

"Don't hit her?" the other responded. "Well I'll show her— teach her a lesson she won't forget." He began to loosen his belt.

"No, not that. Leave her alone. Virgins are worth more. Someone will pay plenty for that privilege in Bangkok."

They fed the girls, retied them, and drugged them. When Martha came to again, she found herself in a dark van or bus with the windows blacked out. Four or five other girls lay trussed up on the floor.

Two drug-hazed days later, men dragged her stumbling into a building. They untied her, stripped her and left her alone with four others. A middle-aged woman entered the room, looked them over with the same gaze a cattle baron would use to evaluate his herd. "Welcome ladies to the Palace of Heavenly Pleasure. We'll get you cleaned up, fed, appropriately dressed, and trained for your new work. In just a few days you can start earning your keep. And don't even think of escaping. When you've been here for a week, not even your mothers will want you back."

***

Martha's mother found her daughter's Bible and one shoe by the roadside and realized what had happened. Someone had grabbed her on the way home from the youth meeting. They immediately contacted Rev. Cha who in turn notified the police and the local opium warlord. Agents of the warlord found the campsite near the Thai border. The Myanmar police worked with the Thai police and followed the trail to Bangkok, but there it went cold.

A mother still pines for her lost child. The official and the unofficial authorities shrug their shoulders, "What can we do?" they ask.

Paul recalls meeting the mother soon after the incident: "She just sat there, stony, motionless, and sad."

Rev. Cha's eyes mist over each time he thinks of the lost child. *We still have much work to do in Myanmar*, he thinks. *Yes, and in Thailand too.*

***

In addition to his commitment to the welfare of children, Cha—initially a businessman who trained for the ministry—also exhibits a natural gift for engineering. He has designed a massive stove to cook food for the Grace Haven home in Lashio and a sewage treatment plant to handle the waste. After passing through a series of septic tanks, the waste runs onto the garden as fertilizer. But the people in the surrounding countryside appreciate his engineering skill for quite another reason.

Medical outreach programs, another part of CNEC's second track, often failed because people returned to their villages, drank polluted water and became seriously ill again. Engineer Cha came to the rescue. Using funds raised overseas for the purpose, he piped clean spring water down mountainsides to storage tanks in the villages.

The grinding poverty and limited opportunities for employment in many Southeast Asia fields of CNEC prompted another critical social program. Most village pastors earn little more than ten US dollars per month. Their parishioners in tribal areas of the Golden Triangle or in West Kalimantan might make no more, often existing by subsistence farming. Since its inception, CNEC never intended that national ministries would continue indefinitely receiving support from Western Christians. They prayed and planned that new ministries would eventually become self-sustaining, and eventually begin supporting other outreach ministries. But how can ministries become self-supporting when the people cannot even afford to feed their children?

As Paul and his co-workers surveyed the many tribal ministries, raising the income of the people seemed an impossible goal. While searching and praying for an answer, they remembered Jesus' words as he looked in compassion on the multitude and said to his disciples, "You give them something to eat."

Jesus in his day solved the problem by miraculously multiplying the loaves and fishes.

CNEC needed a plan that would similarly multiply to meet the needs of the multitudes on the hills and in the valleys of Southeast Asia. In a report to supporters, Paul explained the problem this way: "In under-developed rural and remote villages, the core problem that needs resolution is—How do we respond to those who live in poverty? We cannot tell them who have recently become Christians, 'We will pray for you. May you go in peace!' and then do nothing to help them out of poverty."[82]

The answer came with the micro-enterprise program in which CNEC made available seed money to individuals to begin micro businesses. They set up funds on the field from which local churches, co-workers, and individual Christians can apply for interest-free loans to run small businesses. Business possibilities include raising chickens, goats, pigs or various crops. In a typical situation the new business operator would receive two goats—one male and one female. When the animals reproduce, he or she returns two animals or pays back the seed money, usually the equivalent of one hundred dollars in US funds. CNEC encourages the person to give a small portion of earnings to the fund to insure that it will grow and help many others.

The CNEC national workers responsible for the program in each area suit the business ventures to the local culture and abilities of the individuals or families. One micro-enterprise involves a potato-marketing business. The operator buys potatoes from a grower, washes them, and sells them in the marketplace.

Simon P. Bangun, a CNEC worker in West Kalimantan shared the following in a letter to the Singapore office where staff ably translated it:

Raising goats project has been implemented for a year now. Everything goes on smoothly thus far. In the beginning, we had only eight goats, but now it has increased to 22 goats. More are coming, as some female goats are pregnant and will be due soon. Many non-Christians are envious of us and have expressed their desire to participate in such a project. It's my hope that such a project will extend to non-Christians also so that it may become a contact point to bring them to Christ. . . ."

CHAPTER 15: *Blessings and Perils*

*Matthew 5:45 says ". . . He causes the sun to rise on the evil
and the good, and sends rain on the righteous
and the unrighteous."*

The Changs had never owned a home of their own. Even
throughout the years of raising a family, they lived in whatever
accommodation God provided. In Singapore, government policy
did not permit them as aliens to buy a house or apartment, but
when they became permanent residents, that changed. In 1994
they purchased an apartment or flat in a government-sponsored,
high-rise building[83]—about 80 percent of people in Singapore
live in apartments. In a letter Paul describes it this way: "Our
home is called a three and one-half room flat. It is on the 11th
floor. The elevator goes to the 10th floor, so we walk up one
floor. We have two bedrooms and a hall that extends to the
kitchen. It is compact at about 83 square metres (not quite 900
square feet)."[84]

The hall that they describe is half as wide as the flat and
runs about two-thirds of the length where it becomes a kitchen.
In the middle it bulges to full width between the bedrooms to
create a space suitable for a small living room. The Changs, like
newlyweds in their first home, love it—but they waited decades
to get it. Their letter goes on to describe the great people who
live in the building, including a number in Christian ministry.
They say, "Our vision has been enlarged and our lives enriched."

Meanwhile with Mark and Ruth

As Paul and Nien-chang, still deeply involved in the work of
CNEC, crept into their senior years, their children effectively
established careers and families of their own. At the same time
Mark and Ruth remained strong supporters of their parents,
always ready to answer a family call.

Mark attended Biola University and California State
University at Fullerton to earn a computer degree and now
makes his living in that field. While he strongly supports his

parents and those who do similar work, he has never felt a call from God to follow in their footsteps. He says, "Missionary work was never on my mind. I don't know why. The only thing I could think of was that I could not do what my parents did. I would not be able to come close to what they sacrificed for the gospel. So I dare not try to."

Ruth studied education at Biola University and took a master's program in teaching English as a foreign language at the University of Southern California. In 1994 she married Peter Lam, then a civil engineer. Their daughter, Kaitlin Emily Lam arrived in 1997. Unlike Mark, Ruth had long felt a strong call to missions.

Peril from illness

It seemed like a bomb had burst inside her head—like a massive water main had ruptured beneath the streets of Singapore—like the Day of the Lord had come and the whole earth had begun disintegrating. Nien-chang began to lose her balance. She stumbled toward a checkout counter feeling she might fall with every step. Fighting through a mental mist, she thought, "This occurred once before. What did the doctor tell me to do if it happened again?"

As her body slumped against the checkout counter, she remembered the name of the hospital where Singapore's best brain surgeons worked.

"Madam! Madam, are you all right?"

Someone had spoken to her. The clerk's face came into focus. She felt she had fallen onto the edge of a great abyss; when she tried to move her body refused to respond properly and she fought to keep the contents of her stomach from leaping out onto the checkout counter. Her mind now raced at full speed. Where would Paul be now? Still at home? In the car on his way to work?

"Madam, can you hear me?"

"Yes," Nien-chang answered. At least, her voice worked. "Call the office. Tell them Mrs. Chang is ill." With effort she recited the phone number.

"Sit down; I'll get help," the clerk answered and turned to leave, but Nien-chang stopped her.

"No wait!" she said. "Also call an ambulance to take me to Tan Tock Seng Hospital."

***

"Nien-chang has collapsed at the supermarket," the voice on the phone said. "We've sent a car over, but perhaps you should go too."

Paul moved quickly. Within minutes he arrived at the store just in time to join Nien-chang in the ambulance for the run to the hospital. As the ambulance pushed its way through Singapore traffic, Paul held her hand and prayed. In the hospital she lapsed into unconsciousness.

The gravity of the doctor's voice alone warned Paul of the seriousness of the situation—his words didn't bring any comfort. "A blood vessel in her brain has broken. We cannot yet fully assess the severity of the situation. If she regains consciousness that will be a positive sign."

Paul could do little but pray for a miracle and send out a call for prayer to the Christian community. God answered; the following day Nien-chang regained consciousness. The doctors moved quickly. On Friday, in a four and one-half hour operation, they repaired an aneurism in the brain.

For nearly one month Nien-chang remained in intensive care, but recovered sufficiently to return home soon after. Paul's excitement at God's response to prayer showed in the July/August *Praise and Prayer*:

Mrs. Chang was discharged from the hospital on 16 July, '96, a month after her brain operation for aneurysm on June 14. We thank God for the successful operation and her recovery which doctors said was faster than anyone had expected . . . She is now recuperating at home but will need time to fully regain her speech, memory and mobility . . . However, we praise God that she is already able to do certain things—eating, praying, walking (limited), and even playing the piano!"

Later in a letter to supporters Paul further reflected on the events surrounding that event.

During those days, we also experienced the loving concern of God's children. Using e-mail, greeting cards, prayer letters, and telephone, our loving friends brought us words of encouragement and comfort. That was strength which held us up. Many Christian brothers and sisters cooked and brought us health tonics. Some of them also cooked soups and brought us fruits. Doctors lowered charges, thus helping us to cut down on medical expenses.

There was also a global prayer network formed by many brothers and sisters around the world, both young and old as they prayed for us, A three-year-old girl named Angel heard from her parents that Mrs. Chang was in the hospital. She then went into her room, knelt by her bed and prayed for Mrs. Chang. Another family invited us to dinner in their home every evening for two months, during which time Mrs. Chang was recuperating and not able to cook. God also touched many brothers and sisters to give us money towards our medical expenses.

Our children and their spouses came back from the States, giving us much support. After their mother was discharged from ICU ward and transferred to a regular ward, they returned home to California. Ruth stayed for another two weeks after her mother left the hospital.[85]

Paul ended that letter with a benediction of praise, ". . . He is the sovereign Lord, worthy to be worshipped and loved with all my heart."

Peril on the road

Paul tells this story of a visit to various ministries in Myanmar in May and June of 1999. Chuck Bennett of PI USA and Pastor Chiang Ho Heng (Henry) of CNEC Singapore travelled with him.

Our first stop was the capital Yangon on May 31. Here the Bethel Home was started by Rev. and Mrs. Phun Duma one year ago with ten children. In May 1999, another 37 children were taken in. The objective of the home is to reach out to poor children and orphans with the love of the gospel of Christ. We then took a domestic flight to Mandalay in the north and from here, travelled by road to Lashio.

"Lashio is the birthplace of our first orphanage ministry, the Grace Haven. After almost eight years since its founding by Rev. and Mrs. Cha Tan Yone, it now has about 140 children from various tribes such as Lisu, Lahu, Miao, Yao, and Chinese.

"From Lashio we proceeded to Maymyo (near Mandalay) where we have several partner ministries-Sheng Dao Bible School, Trinity Lisu Bible School, Lisu Baptist Bible College, and an Operation Dawn drug rehabilitation centre.[86]

"We were on the last leg of our visit . . ."[87]

***

When Chuck Bennett seated himself in Cha's car as they prepared to leave Maymyo for Mandalay, he felt the hard lump against his upper leg and realized he had sat on his seat belt. "A bad idea," he thought as he fished it out. "Not that it matters—I got the broken one anyway."

He tucked it into the crack between the seat and backrest as the other three men piled into the old Toyota Land Cruiser. Feeling like a mother nagging reluctant children, Chuck said, "Don't forget to do up your seat belts."

He watched at least one pair of shoulders shrug in resignation, but he also noticed that three pairs of hands fumbled for the lost belt ends. "So if it takes nagging to make three grown men think about safety, I'll nag," he thought as the car pulled away. He wondered, "How many times have I reminded people to fasten their seat belts? Thousands of times? How often did I lean back from the pilot's seat and tug on seat belts around children, and even adults, just to make sure they had fastened them correctly?"

During his 30 years—much of that time as a pilot—with Missionary Aviation Fellowship, Chuck had made over 18,000 flights, many over mountains and jungle, but he realized few of those trips would equal in danger this six- or seven-hour trip from Lashio to Mandalay. They now had only the Maymyo to Mandalay leg to go—about an hour's drive. The second-rate surface, winding road, hairpin turns, occasional crazy driver, and Myanmar's strange practice of using right-hand drive cars on the right side of the road made journeys of any length unsafe.

Chuck watched Rev. Cha at the wheel. He looked inconsequential, but he drove well. Looks could fool. Chuck knew that behind that quiet exterior and retiring personality lived a capable leader who had proven himself as a pastor, administrator, and practical engineer. Chuck shifted his attention to Paul, sitting stoically beside the driver. *He's in the death seat,* thought Chuck. *The one who sits beside the driver gets the worst in a crash. Pastor Henry Chiang and I in the back have the safest seats—even without a seat belt. But why can't I get my mind on things other than safety?*

Chuck shifted his thoughts back to Paul. *Cha may be steering this car, but Paul is driving this trip.* He remembered how Paul had talked him into coming against his own better judgement. Anyway, it had been a great experience—he had learned much even though he would retire soon and not make great use of the knowledge. *Paul is a born leader. He leads by the sheer force of his personality. If you're on Paul's team, you'd better lean into the traces and pull in the same direction.*

The Land Cruiser continued on, bumping over uneven

pavement and swaying around sharp curves. The passengers
either chatted in Mandarin—switching occasionally to English
for Chuck's sake—tried to snooze, or watched the beautiful
countryside. Time moved slowly, but they would soon reach
Mandalay.

Chuck didn't see it coming—or if he did he doesn't remember. The approaching vehicle swung wide on a curve and they
struck head on. He remembers Singapore four days later and he
recalls learning through a wall of confusion that they would not
continue the trip to China.

Paul filled him in on the details.

The force of the crash propelled Chuck into the front seat,
where he bounced off Paul and struck his head against the dash-
board. Paul's shoulder belt broke a rib but likely saved his life.

Following the scream of tires, the deafening crash, the
moan of a dying car, the stabbing pain, and a moment of
stunned silence, Paul stumbled from the wreck, an arm across
his chest to ease the pain. He flagged down a passing small
truck. The driver immediately offered to take them into the hospital in Mandalay. He carried a cell[88] phone, not a common
practice in Myanmar. At Paul's request, he phoned ahead to
Rev. Paul Liu at the Methodist Church in Mandalay asking him
to meet them at the hospital. When given the request, the driver
looked at Paul in surprise and said, "I know that church; I'm not
a Christian, but my brother-in-law is, and he attends it."

The three less-seriously injured travellers helped Chuck into
the cab of the tiny pickup truck beside the driver and climbed
into the back. The trip to the hospital in normal circumstances
would have taken 45 minutes, but the driver, concerned for his
hurting passengers, drove slowly to avoid the bumps and ease
the discomfort of the curves.

Rev. Paul Liu met them at the hospital and helped speed
them through the formalities. The doctor taped up Paul and
stitched Chuck's lacerated head wound. Only then did Paul and
the others realize the seriousness of Chuck's injury and thank
God he hadn't bled to death along the way. The doctor signed
Chuck into the hospital and took a CAT scan but failed to notice

Chuck's fractured skull.

Two days later the hospital released the patient allowing all three travellers to fly to Yangon and on to Singapore.

Jane, Chuck's wife, heard of the accident and managed to get through to them in Yangon. Paul assured her that her husband's head wound was healing and he was just overtired. But she became alarmed when Chuck could not carry on a conversation—he simply repeated her name. She flew immediately to Singapore to take charge of him where doctors informed her of the seriousness of her husband's fractured skull.

Paul Chang, Rev. Cha, and Pastor Henry Chiang recovered from their injuries without long-term problems, but Chuck still suffers from hearing, balance, and neck problems. All now appreciate even more the danger of travelling in remote areas with only limited medical help nearby. Thankfully, the Great Physician had accompanied them as the unseen fifth passenger.

***

Paul's Myanmar crash was not the first car accident for a member of the Chang family.

Mark Chang tells us: "One year when we travelled to the States to do deputation work for a year, we had a rear-end collision (we stopped, the other car hit us at highway speed). Our station wagon exploded. None of us received serious injury. But the most important thing to me was that my parents did not even think of suing the driver. My dad told me that the lawyer or insurance agent came to the office sweating, thinking that we would ask for thousands. I didn't understand it at that time (I was seven or eight) but now I do. If God protected us from that fiery inferno, how much more would He watch over us in our daily lives."

CHAPTER 16: *The Work Goes On*

*Confucius said, "Good people should be
slow to speak but quick to act."*

The Southeast Asia field continued to expand under Paul's leadership. In 1996 Paul had made an exploratory trip to Cambodia, describing that land in colourful terms.

> Cambodia! Cambodia! I cry with you. After I stepped out of the plane in Phnom Penh, I got into a 30-year-old Mercedes Benz and was driven to the place I was to stay for a few days.
>
> The streets were full of homeless children—skinny, ragged and filthy. There were many people without limbs. It was reported one out of every two hundred Cambodians is handicapped because of mines. On both sides of the street, there are crowded nightclubs with signs in Khmer, Chinese and English enticing tourists to enter.
>
> I talked to the people, visited the museum and the area where the torture centre used to be, and the monument of the *killing fields*. These still live in the hearts of the Cambodians—when they talk to you, they tell how and when they lost their family members.
>
> Pray for God's care and love to heal the Cambodians' wounds and that their lives would be mended.[89]

CNEC began working with existing Christian groups in Cambodia and in 1999 established the Crossroads Student Centre in Phnom Penh. This student hostel opened with 12 young men, university students, under the leadership of Rev. Wati Longkumer, a missionary from Nagaland, India. A year later, a missionary couple, David Ooi and Moonjung Nam, took over the Crossroads Centre. David and Moonjung come with unique qualifications. David, an ethnic Chinese from Malaysia,

studied in Singapore and the UK. He trained as a barrister and
practiced law for three years. At age 20 he began volunteering
with CNEC, but felt a call to full-time mission work and attended
Columbia International University, South Carolina. There he
met Moonjung, a Korean-American.

When Paul visited them, he reported:

> July 24, 2001 is a day for celebration because nine uni-
> versity students of Cambodia Universities are baptised.
> They are filled with joy and praise because they are the
> first batch of students from Crossroads Student Centre!
> David and Moon spent one whole year's time living
> together with them every day. Their lives testify to
> God's love and they also taught them God's Word.
> These students also come from Buddhist families, but
> they are baptized! All of them confessed the Lord Jesus
> Christ as their personal Saviour and Lord. God also
> brought a few new students into their midst.[90]

James Lai in Malaysia
The work in Malaysia grew rapidly under the leadership of
James Lai—by the year 2000, most of the churches had become
self-supporting and the tribal work had extended into ten
groups. Directing the Partners Training Centre, overseeing the
Good News Correspondence Course office, and leading the
ministries in Malaysia keeps him busy. But he still finds time to
travel to restricted areas to preach evangelistic messages and
break new ground. Even with his heavy schedule, he has managed to work toward a doctoral program in missiology.

His excitement about his work comes through in this report:

> I would like to share with you some of the excitement
> that our God has made happen here among the Orang
> Laut people. The Orang Laut are a small, unreached
> people group numbering approximately seven thousand
> that live in the slum villages along the coasts of west
> Malaysia, many of which can only be reached by boat.

Most of the people come from animistic backgrounds, but we are seeing many of this people group come to know the Lord. Worship services among the adults and children are carried out regularly every Sunday in three villages. . . . Earlier this year, 15 people were baptized. Two buildings (each able to accommodate around one hundred people) were built, as the old smaller ones became weak. Praise the Lord who blessed the ministry with a van, which is very useful.

***

In 2002, James Lai supplied a guide to take a visiting journalist to an Orang Laut or Sea Dayak tribal village near the City of Johor Bahru, just across the Strait of Johor from Singapore. The following report ensued.

***

We drove a few hundred metres beyond a modern subdivision, stopped in an isolated waterfront parking lot, and began walking to a secluded settlement to visit the Sea Dayak people. We passed along a dirt pathway beside overgrown grasslands and mangrove thickets and followed elevated, rickety walkways above tidal washes filled with litter from sea and land.

The "village" stretched along the waterfront with unpainted wooden shacks standing on poles above a littered beach. With the tide out, the seaward sides of the huts barely extended over the water's edge; with the tide in, the sea would rise almost to the floors of the homes and lap against the path on which we stood.

We had reached a settlement of 21 families. A dozen years ago, it had remained hidden from the nearby city, caught in a time warp, and ignored—if not rejected—by the government.

The Sea Dayaks, as opposed to Land Dayaks who live inland, had fled before encroaching development and eventually stopped at the Johor Strait where they settled on a remote shoreline. There they eked out a subsistence living with shallow-water fishing.

Again, civilization and urban sprawl threatened. The Dayaks took the worst from it, succumbing to alcohol, while governments rejected or ignored them and withheld social programs. Neighbours despised them. Addiction, disease, and poverty took them to early graves. But somehow, nearly naked, illiterate, threatened by encroaching development, and living in fear, they managed to cling to their wretched home sites.

Then Pastor Charles found them. For the last 12 years he has dedicated his life to the Sea Dayaks.

Now most of the people have escaped alcoholism. They have revived their fishing careers and send their children to school so that ignorance and illiteracy won't enslave the next generation. They have exchanged their rags for presentable clothing and, with help from their tireless benefactor, seek medical care. Electrical power now lights their homes and makes life easier.

Glimpsing inside their houses, we saw sleeping mats on the floors and very few pieces of furniture, but television sets and radios occupied key places. We visited with a family who had three children born with clubfeet, but each in different stages of surgical correction. A young fisherman resting after a morning of work had a cell phone clipped to his shorts to give instant access to the middleman who buys the daily catch.

In a world filled with too many examples of man's inhumanity to man, I thought you'd like to read the good news.

Even though governments and society often turn their backs, isn't it great to live in a world favoured with great heros like Charles?[91]

***

When the board of CNEC Southeast Asia cast about for a replacement for Paul Chang, the lot fell to James Lai.

Some things never change

"The pickup groaned as its wheels tried to climb the slopes towards Hwei Mei Ling. The ground was muddy and slippery after a downpour the previous night. Making our way uphill included shovelling mud from under the wheels, pushing and treading on mud. It took us three hours before we finally reached our destination," wrote Paul following one of his numerous mission trips to a remote village. It might have happened during any of the last four decades or even last week. If you substitute a handcart or a train for the truck, it could describe one of the hundreds of journeys that occurred throughout Paul's seven decades.

Much in the same way as the book of *Acts* tells the continuing and unending story of the apostles as they built bridges to every corner of the globe, the stories of the Chang family and of CNEC Southeast Asia continue. As the apostles followed in Jesus' steps, they equipped others to take their places in turn. As James Lai completes work on a doctoral program and prepares to assume the leadership of CNEC Southeast Asia, Ruth Chang begins her ministry in China as a third-generation Chang missionary.

CHAPTER 17 : *Defining A Modern-day Apostle*

The Apostle Paul said, "Here is a trustworthy saying:
if any one sets his heart on being an overseer,
he desires a noble task."[92]

A world perspective

Not everyone who says, "Yes Lord, I will follow you," lives a life like Paul Chang.

Not all sons and daughters of great Christian leaders follow in their parents' footsteps. Not every escapee who flees through enemy lines gets an opportunity to return to the enemy camp as a welcome visitor. Not all of us who have opportunity to study, turn that advantage into multiple undergraduate and graduate degrees. Not everyone who sings, persists with voice training and gets an offer from a major operatic society. Most of us who set lofty goals, rarely reach them.

What makes Chang Bao-wha the youth and the Reverend Dr. Paul Chang the adult stand out from the crowd? What propelled him from obscurity to a position akin to that of a modern-day apostle?

Some would say the genes determine it all. As our opening chapters indicate, Paul was born in a great province of a great nation. The people of Shandong grew large in stature and often exhibited significant creative and leadership qualities.

Others would identify centuries of a complex culture as the prime factor. Those of us from the Western world rarely appreciate the great and numerous contributions of China to the world. With a calculating smile on his face, Paul would identify Chinese cooking as a key gift to the world—many westerners would agree.

Students of psychology might argue that personality is the main factor in determining success, suggesting that the right combination of ego and self-image drive winners to the top of the heap.

Committed Christians and students of God's Word would vote for a sound education in the Bible and a sensitivity to the voice of the Holy Spirit as decisive factors. They would argue that only 'purpose-driven' lives—provided those purposes come from God—can make people all God intends them to be. And we must never forget the influence of the prayers of dedicated mothers.

Without a doubt, all of the above are apparent in the life of Paul Chang. But how we evaluate those things depends on our own background.

A Western co-worker (American) and friend of Paul has said, "Paul Chang is certainly a complex—almost paradoxical—person. Heroic, committed, talented, charming. But he can also be controlling and domineering."

An Eastern co-worker (ethnic Chinese) and friend said, "Paul is my father. He acts with care and concern, leading in the same way a good father leads his family." Another Chinese co-worker said. "I know Paul as a mentor, friend, visionary and an untiring and fearless warrior. Although he is not a leader without flaws and weaknesses, his strengths always outshine and cover his shortcomings."

Two hemispheres—slightly different points of view.

The book *Temperament and the Christian Faith*[93] by O. Hallesby breaks the temperaments of people into four main classifications—an evaluation of personality types that has existed since Roman times. The theory has value because individuals can often fit themselves or others into specific categories and learn the strengths and weaknesses of each personality type.

Paul Chang fits into the classification known as *choleric.* Hallesby claims that people with a choleric temperament are strong willed; they want to make all decisions concerning themselves and for all others whose lives touch theirs. They immediately see answers to problems and press forward, usually in a practical fashion. They act quickly and boldly in emergencies, undismayed by adversity or the objection of others.

They have another side. Their tendency to appear impetuous, self-confident, and domineering often alienates lesser people. But they usually end up on the winning side for their energy and drive enables them to accomplish their goals regardless of what others think.

The Apostle Paul is the Bible's best-known choleric. Paul Chang like his namesake shows most of the characteristics of a choleric. Some students of personality and leadership would prefer to classify Paul as a *Type* A personality.

Observers from a North American or European perspective, steeped in western values that have come down to us from the Greeks and Romans and modified by centuries of Christianity, should realize Chinese culture and history differ greatly. This means that personality and leadership styles also differ. In Chinese society, leadership styles centre about traditional Confucian values with paternalism appearing as a strong characteristic. Paternalism relates directly to the Confucian values of respect for authority, conformity, and deference. Eastern values that shape leadership style at times conflict with those common in the West. All need to remember that Eastern and Western values and culture do not necessarily conflict with biblical principles.

We cannot judge or understand the lives of people from other cultures if we insist on evaluating them while wearing the blinkers of our own culture.

Again, let us appeal to the Apostle Paul. Can you think of another New Testament leader with a more paternalistic leadership style?

A family perspective
Whatever our culture, living within a missionary family presents challenges that most people would find difficult. But it does present opportunities for growth that not all appreciate. Paul learned to preach, teach, and evangelize at his father's side. He suffered separation from family and country in order to follow in his father's footsteps. He views his father, Chang Hsueh Kung, the way the world does—as a hero of the faith, a man God used in his time, a person willing to become a martyr for Jesus Christ. But for the first few years of his life, he saw him up close as a son sees a father.

Now Paul has a son and daughter who have watched him

and evaluated his lifestyle for almost four decades.

His daughter Ruth says: "My dad is a man of faith. He didn't say much to us about his childhood, especially after he left his family and home and had to rely on himself and God. But I know he has tremendous faith. When I was very young, I spied my dad kneeling on the floor next to the bed talking to God. Parents can tell you as a child, to pray, to love God, and obey Him, but I saw my parents modelling an authentic relationship with the Lord."

Ruth also identifies her mother as a major influence in her life. "I learned a lot about my parents' relationship with Jesus by observing the time they spent meeting with Him. Mom always has a journal in her hand and takes notes about many things she reads in the Scripture and hears in sermons. She even takes notes till this day of Dad's preaching—and she's been following him everywhere for 38 years! At a tender age, I learned from my dad and mom that God is a real, living friend—someone you need to spend time with."

Ruth also learned to develop relationships with earthly friends. "Ever since I can remember, we had guests in our home—people from villages, people from big cities. We had Americans, Indians, Thai, Australians, Africans, and more. They often brought interesting gifts: carved wooden animals from Africa, cloth from a tribal area, or chocolate from America. It was exciting, listening to stories and learning about unusual practices in other cultures. My dad and mom have the gift of helps and generosity. So, I learned at a young age to be a good hostess."

Entertaining costs money. Those who work in the field of human relations, tell us that money contributes more to damaged interpersonal relationships than any other factor. Missionaries do have human tendencies and problems occur even among those who have dedicated themselves to serving God.

Paul and Nien-chang appear to have escaped the money trap. Mark says: "I remember finding out how much my dad made. It upset me that Partners International paid him so little. I don't think he had a raise in 15 years (he would never ask for one). I found out that he made something like $30,000 a year for a very long time. In my first job, I made twice as much as he did! However, from this I realize that my dad never intended to get rich—as many in ministry do."

But living in the Chang missionary family had other real drawbacks as Ruth points out. "As a family we couldn't easily or openly talk about negative or uncomfortable things. From the time I was two to fifteen, I lived in ten different places and three locations in the world. It took me almost 15 years as an adult, to come to grips with my grief of loss and the feeling of abandonment."

Paul recalls how he, rather belatedly, became aware of his daughter's lonely battle with the missionary lifestyle. A church in California asked the Chang family to form a panel and allow the audience to question them about the missionary life. Paul felt a sense of pride when their now-adult children took seats beside their parents on the platform. The panel went well until someone aimed a question at Ruth.

"Ruth, how did you as a child feel as a missionary kid?"

Ruth pulled out all the stops, articulately describing feelings of abandonment, loneliness, loss of friends and culture, and dis-orientation with every move from house to house and country to country. The revelation stunned Paul. Why had he not heard all this before? Had he been blind and unfeeling? Had he neglected his family? Or had he, like so many other missionaries been caught in a missionary culture trap? His eyes misted and he knew one thing for certain: he really loved his son and daughter.

Ruth agrees, "My parents love the Lord and their children. But, like many families, and especially missionary families in the earlier days, they had little information on transition, loss, and cultural disorientation. My family did not process these things well. They just understood that you follow the Lord and you do your best. I wished it had been different, but I am who I am because of my experiences. I don't regret one minute of my life and I would probably not change much of it. I learned through living in the Chang family that it is okay for people in missionary work to grieve when they lose their familiar surroundings, the people they love, other things that give stability. Experiencing grief and needing space to deal with life transitions and losses is normal. In fact, if you embrace it, you become more capable of dealing in a healthier way with change, loss, and difficulty."

Today Ruth and her husband Peter work among the poor in China as poverty-relief workers. Why is she there? She would tell you that she and her husband, Peter, came to this land because of Jesus and the influence of family.

She says, "My grandfather was a martyr for Christ. His life and suffering remind me of the Lord who came to suffer and die so that people might live. I want to follow the path of my destiny God started in my grandfather. My parents modeled for me what it means to love people that are not your own, who are of a different culture. They embraced them into their lives and into their homes. My dad modeled faith and a great learning posture.

"He's gone through so much in his life—as a refugee, leaving his family, being poor and alone—yet, he has a real big heart to love and to show compassion, and to be used by Him. My mother embodies gentleness and patience. From her, I have learned that in treating people, I need more patience and must exhibit more grace. All that my parents are and what they have taught me, has brought me to the place I am today. Without them and their lives, I would probably never have been open to being a poverty-relief worker."

EPILOGUE: *Building Cultural Bridges in the 21st Century*

Arthur O'Shaughnessy said,
"We are the music makers,
And we are the dreamers of dreams, . . .
Yet we are the movers and shakers
Of the world forever, it seems."

Even as Paul Chang prepares to retire from his leadership role and assume different responsibilities, the team he has built presses ahead in the mission fields that have remained central in Paul's life for 30 years. The following summary does not include all of the partner ministries working with CNEC in Southeast Asia, only those specifically mentioned in the preceding chapters. Consider all numbers approximate—they change from day to day.

West Kalimantan
The annual report[94] from the CNEC West Kalimantan ministries for 2002 glowed with a sense of optimism. The work in this province of Indonesia began like the other CNEC ministries in Southeast Asia—first to the Chinese, then to the tribes, then to the nation as a whole. The report speaks of evangelism among ethnic Chinese, tribal peoples, and Muslims, thus representing all segments of the Indonesian population.

They also report another development that speaks of the maturity of the work. The leaders of the ministry made several trips to Jakarta, Indonesia's capital, to present the needs of the work to the churches there. They say: "The biggest support came from a church in Jakarta. They sponsored 70 per cent of the building expenses for two classrooms of Seti Bakti Secondary School. They had partnered with us in various ways: providing rice monthly for the teachers, giving bursaries to some students, supporting renovating expenses, and providing facilities for learning and teaching."

In addition they reported the following:
- · number who received short-term training   300
- · number of children sponsored   796
- · number of children in orphanages   20
- · number of associated churches   84
- · number of pastors and workers   68

They indicated that one hundred, nineteen people had become Christians and the membership of the associated churches had passed seven thousand—evidence that the bridge to the mountain works!

Myanmar, Shan State

The Reverend Cha Tan Yone and his wife Susan continue to lead the work in Shan State in northeastern Myanmar. By the end of 2002 CNEC records indicated that the ministry sponsored 1,375 children living in various communities in Shan State while Grace Haven Ministry—operating homes in seven locations—housed 442 orphaned, needy, or abandoned children. The children in the homes come from a number of cultural and tribal backgrounds. In these refuges, caring Christian workers minister to their intellectual, physical, and spiritual needs until they can resume a normal life in the community. Rev. Cha reports: "About 95 per cent of the children in our centres have put their faith in Christ. Praise the Lord! Some of the children come from Christian families and they too experience changed lives. We hope that one day these children will return to their home village and win their tribe to Christ."

Mid 2003 saw at least two young people from Grace Haven studying in Bible colleges. Also, the Miao Student Centre operates a three-month Bible class (in the Miao language) for young people interested in full-time Christian service. Nine students attend the classes, some from Grace Haven homes and others from the villages—it appears that Rev. Cha's 'hope' will soon become a reality.

The Pastors Training Centre in Lashio runs Bible training classes in the Miao and Chinese languages.

CNEC in Myanmar has taken the concept of establishing student centres where students can live while studying away from home to another level by opening a university student centre in Mandalay. A large house will become the residence for eight to ten university students from various CNEC churches in Myanmar. After a time of discipling the students, the centre, known as Hope of Mandalay Student Centre, will take in non-Christian students as an evangelistic thrust.

There are now 25 churches and 65 pastors and Christian workers associated with the CNEC ministry in the Shan State. The Holy Light Church in Lashio alone, has about 400 worshippers on Sundays. Students in The Holy Light School number approximately 1400.

Myanmar, Chin State
For many years the children's home in Yangon (formerly, Rangoon), used space on the upper floors of a near-derelict building. In 2002 an American supporter visited the Reverend Phun Duma and his wife K. Nawni who lead the ministry there. When he saw the difficult living conditions experienced by the children, he funded the purchase of a new acreage outside the city and the construction of a new building.

The workers use various means to reach out to children in Chin State. Their report for 2002 indicates the Sponsor-a-Child ministry held numerous children's camps. A report from only two of them indicated that out of 300 children, 93 received Christ as their saviour.

At the end of 2002 CNEC sponsored 242 children in Chin State and by mid 2003 Bethel Home housed 59 children. There are now 72 churches, 81 pastors and Christian workers, and 19 office staff associated with the CNEC ministry in the Chin State.

Cambodia
A report by David and Moonjung Ooi issued in 2003 highlighted these interesting points:
- In 1992, just before the United Nations entered and aided Cambodia, there were as few as 20 churches in the country.
- In early 2000 a newspaper report suggested that 85 per

cent of believers were 'rice Christians'.

· In 2001, the Evangelical Fellowship of Cambodia reported that there were 6,000 churches in Cambodia.

With this appalling statistic suggesting such a high percentage of rice Christians, CNEC Southeast Asia leadership established The Crossroads ministry. The Crossroads would seek to train and equip university students to become future leaders in the Cambodian church. They do it by welcoming university students to the residence. All students in residence must participate in leadership training and character-developing programs. These students attend the Crossroads Church and reach out to others. The church upholds the concept of life-influence-life principle that helps in penetrating the gospel barrier in Cambodia—a nation that hates and isolates Christianity.

The Crossroads Student Centre has two full-time workers and one affiliated church. CNEC sponsors no children in Cambodia.

Thailand

In a report dated June 2003, the Reverend Boonprasert Vijitrakul and his wife Boon Har reported 43 residents—33 males and 10 females—in the New Vision drug rehabilitation centre near Chiangmai. The success of this ministry has given it a good reputation in the community and among government agencies.

Boonprasert says, "Most of the inhabitants are under 30 years of age. Each has his or her own drug of choice, including heroin, opium, ecstasy, tranquilizers, liquor, and even glue. Most have little education or none at all."

CNEC sponsors 980 children in northern Thailand to encourage intellectual, social, and spiritual growth. By equipping Sunday school teachers through training, they provide spiritual leaders for children in remote areas. The training facility in Chiangmai runs the Sunday school teacher-training programs, youth training camps, short term training for Christian workers, and specialized training for women from the hill areas. A student centre in Chiangrai houses 23 students.

There are now 26 CNEC affiliated churches and 45 pastors and Christian workers associated with the CNEC partner ministries in Thailand.

Malaysia

CNEC affiliated churches that minister to the ethnic Chinese have worked for many years in Malaysia, but government policy prohibits conversions among the predominately Muslim population. The CNEC Malaysia regional office carries on an extensive training and publishing ministry among the Chinese believers.

They have targeted tribal groups such as the Orang Laut, also known as the Sea Dayaks, who have not espoused Islam. Even this can attract official interference as this report for 2002 reveals:

> A sad incident occurred a few months ago. The Orang Laut chief and a few villagers visited the trusted men of the Sultan (State Royalty) to discuss lumbering. The officials were very angry to know that some villagers had become Christians. They threatened that the Sultan might cut their benefits such as housing allowances, water, and power supply. They must believe in Islam, not Christianity. The chief returned and advised his people to forsake their faith in order to please the Sultan. He also ordered the CNEC workers to leave the village. Though some Christians forsook their faith, five families remained faithful to God. They said, "We will follow Christ no matter what."

In another area they reported that the Orang Laut had begun tithing. There are 24 CNEC workers and pastors in Malaysia and 36 affiliated churches.

China

Most of the CNEC work carried on in China comes under the CNEC East Asia field with Dr. Ben Sia as coordinator. However, Paul and others from CNEC Southeast Asia have made frequent trips into China and established relationships with Christian groups there. For security reasons, they release very little information about the number of workers or affiliated churches. CNEC Southeast Asia does sponsor a number of children in one province in China.

***

At the time of publication, the CNEC Southeast Asia office has eight staff workers.

APPENDICES

Appendix 1: Chinese History

Chinese Dynasties and Republics	Dates	Chinese Historical Events	Biblical and Christian Contemporary Events
Pottery Cultures Yang-shao Lung-shan	4000-1700 BC 2000-1850 BC		Abraham and the patriarchs
Shang	1700-1100 BC	Developed full-fledged urban societies on the sites of older villages.	Israel in Egypt The Exodus
Zhou Western Zhou Eastern Zhou Spring & Autumn Period	1100-221 BC 1100-771 BC 770-256 BC 770-476 BC	"Mandate of heaven" emerged as a political concept—heaven approves good rulers. Socially, they accepted Chinese superiority.	Time of the Judges David and Solomon The Divided Kingdom Captivity & Return
Warring States Period	476-221 BC	Confucius lived and landlord class evolved.	Old Testament closes
Qin	221-207 BC	China united for first time; Great Wall built. Standardized writing, coinage, weights and measures.	

			Christ on earth Early church
Han Western Han Eastern Han	206 BC-AD 220 206 BC-AD 24 AD 25-AD 220	Modern state founded Confucianism adopted as the state norm	
Three Kingdoms Period Wei Shu Han Wu	220-280 220-265 221-263 222-280	Invasion by neighbours and great migrations of Chinese people.	
Jin Western Jin Eastern Jin	265-420 265-316 317-420		Conversion of Constantine (312)
Southern & Northern Dynasties **Southern** Song Qi Liang Chen **Northern** Northern Wei Eastern Wei Western Wei Northern Qi Northern Zhou	420-589 420-479 479-502 502-557 557-589 386-534 534-550 535-556 550-577 557-581	Buddhism grew in popularity. Some northerners absorbed into Chinese culture.	
Sui	581-618	China reunited. Canal building began. Nestorian Christians established in China.	

Dynasty	Dates	Description	World Events
Tang	618-907	Considered as the golden age of power and prosperity.	Nestorian missionaries arrive in China via the Silk Route (635).
Five Dynasties Later Liang Later Tang Later Jin Later Han Later Zhou	907-960 907-923 923-936 936-946 947-950 951-960	Split into independent states, but economic growth continued.	
Liao	916-925		
Song Northern Song Southern Song	960-1279 960-1127 1127-1279	Genghis Khan began the Mongol invasions. Took . Beijing	
Western Xia	1038-1227		The Crusades
Jin	1115-1234		
Yuan (Mongol)	1271-1368	Mongols took south China under Kublai Khan. Promoted trade with outsiders.	Catholics invited to China; established church.
Ming	1368-1644	Drove back Mongols. Buddhism and Taoism made state religions. Descended into turmoil.	Martin Luther (1517) Catholics send Ricci and other missionaries to China (1583)

Qing (Manchu)	1644-1911	Manchus invaded and seized power. Prosperity returned, but China remained inward-looking. Westerners arrived. British sold opium to Chinese, but when Chinese resisted, opium wars began. China opened to trade. Taiping and Boxer rebellions occurred.	Catholics expelled Protestant missionary societies entered China Catholics reopened their missions
Chinese Republics Republic of China	1912-1949	China a republic in name only. Various forces vied for north. Communist party founded. Nationalist Party controlled south. Cooperation between Nationalists and communists ceased—war ensued. Japanese invaded.	
People's Republic of China	1949-	Mao proclaimed the People's Republic of China.	Many missionaries left—CNEC* founded Missionaries expelled from China

* Then known as Chinese Native Evangelistic Crusade—Founded in 1943.

Appendix 2: Dr. John Kao

When John was a teenager, he and his family made a last-minute escape to Hong Kong when the Communists took over mainland China in 1949. Earlier in 1948, his mother (Mrs. Dorcas Kao) became a Christian through the ministry of Mr. A. E. Phillips, a Brethren missionary from England, while the family was living in Kiangxi Province. After the family had moved to Hong Kong, John gave his life to the Lord and was baptized with his parents on Easter Sunday, 1950, at the Kowloon City Baptist Church.

During a time when John was seriously ill from tuberculosis, he felt the Lord's call to full-time Christian service. After overcoming many obstacles, he entered CNEC's Hong Kong Bible College in 1952. In 1962 he earned a Master of Religious Education Degree (M.R.E.) from the Biblical Seminary in New York. Allen Finley invited him to return to Hong Kong to teach in the Hong Kong Bible College. For the next 30 years, John continued serving the Lord while pursuing his studies in Hong Kong, Canada, and the USA, culminating in a Doctor of Ministry degree from Trinity Evangelical Divinity School. During most of these years, John had been associated with CNEC/Partners International.

In 1969, John and Esther and their two sons emigrated to Canada. Allen Finley invited them to do deputational ministry for CNEC throughout North America on behalf of national co-workers. During a deputational engagement at the 1972 World Missions Conference in Jackson, Mississippi, John's message and his enthusiasm and burden for world missions greatly impressed Dr. Paul B. Smith. Dr. Smith invited John to share his testimony with his congregation at The Peoples Church in Toronto. Since then, John has spoken there regularly.

During his deputation years, he visited more than one hundred large and small churches in southeastern United States, sharing the ministry of CNEC and raising support for national workers and Sponsor-a-Child programs. But he paid close attention to speakers from other missions, and learned practical lessons in church planting and church growth.

In the fall of 1974, John returned to Southeast Asia, where CNEC, under the leadership of Dr. Andrew Song, commissioned him to plant churches among Chinese communities in North America. After John and Esther returned to Toronto in December, 1974, they and six other Christian couples sought God's will in planting a church in Toronto. With CNEC assistance, they founded the Toronto Chinese Community Church in Toronto's mid-town on January 12, 1975. John received partner assistance from CNEC for the first two years only and quickly reversed the process by establishing a missions budget.

For the past 28 years, the Toronto Chinese Community Church has grown and planted seven other Chinese churches in the Toronto area with total Sunday attendance approaching six thousand. The churches have banded together under the name Association of Chinese Evangelical Ministries (ACEM). Joint annual world missions giving for the eight congregations now exceeds one million Canadian dollars.

John adds: "I have served as the founder, senior pastor and general director for many years. Since taking up the position of general secretary of the Chinese Coordination Centre of World Evangelism in July 2001, my position is now the founder and consulting pastor of the ACEM. Through many years of association with CNEC/Partners International. I am filled with joy and thanksgiving to celebrate their 60th anniversary."

Appendix 3: Pastor David Soo

David Soo was born Soo Hiu Zheng in Yunnan Province, China, on April 9, 1916. He married and had two daughters and might have lived out his life in his home village had the tremendous upheavals in Chinese history not overtaken him.

In 1942 he joined the Nationalist Chinese army when the Japanese army invaded. The further battles between Nationalist and Communist forces tore Chinese society apart—the China he knew disintegrated. David escaped death when Japanese forces attacked his home village, but became very ill. When his comrades could no longer carry him, they left him to die in an abandoned house. There he had a near-death experience, when an unearthly messenger that he later identified as an angel from God, spoke to him, "Rest assured, you will not die. Peace be with you."

In 1945 following the Japanese surrender, David became a teacher in his home town. His new career didn't last long. The civil war ended in favour of the Communists and David, like many of his countrymen—especially those who had fought with the Nationalists—fled across the southern border. In Burma he joined an exiled army to discourage the Red Army from entering Burma. Ultimately, he settled in Thailand.

He could not return to China and after a few years when reunion with his wife and family seemed impossible, he married a Yao tribal woman. In 1967 David responded to the gospel message through the ministry of Grace Chang, a CNEC missionary of Chinese descent. Encouraged by Grace Chang and the Reverend John Lu, the Southeast Asia field director, David began assuming more responsibility.

After testing his gift of evangelism among the Chinese community and tribal people, David opted to move to Hwei Hai, 40 kilometres north of Chiangrai on the edge of the infamous Golden Triangle. Here he would begin by evangelizing people from his own part of China, then reach out to others. He established Hwei Hai Holy Grace Church and used it as a base to reach into the Golden Triangle. He hiked for great distances through the wooded hills, reaching both Chinese and tribal communities. He successfully walked a narrow line, preaching an uncompromising gospel and yet remaining on agreeable terms with warlords who controlled many of the villages, and the Thai government officials who vied for authority.

For the remainder of his life, as long as health permitted, he continued walking the hills, evangelizing and establishing churches, schools, and orphanages. He retired in ill health to Chiangmai in March of 1989 and died one year later.

Appendix 4: Dr. Paul Chang on Communism

When Paul first returned to China in 1979, 30 years after leaving, he could see no improvements made by the Communists since his childhood. They had taken over the properties of "imperialists" in places like Shanghai, but had let them go to ruins. Most of all, he noticed that the poor had remained poor.

Paul believes that God permitted the Communists to take over China as a means of preparing the people to hear the gospel. They put the church through severe persecution, and found that the people were willing to die for the cause of Christ. It proved to the authorities that Christianity wasn't just a Western religion. Now the government no longer calls them "dogs of imperialism."

Paul argues that the Communists did three main things that helped the church.

They destroyed the family bond: They split up families, separating them into male and female dormitories. While this attempt to modify the social structure created great hardship, it did ravage the Chinese practice of ancestral worship.

They unified the language: They declared Mandarin the national language, meaning that local dialects lost importance. Today you can communicate in Mandarin throughout the country.

They dispersed the church: Many Christians fled to Hong Kong, Singapore, and other places outside mainland China. In their new homes they established churches and schools and began to evangelize their neighbours. Chinese people from the dispersion are now reaching back into their homeland.

China has changed since Paul's historic return. While the people have better incomes and lifestyle, they appear to have no moral foundation—money has become the main motivator. Society has become less civil; as people scramble to do better, they have become rude and self-centred. People generally do not marry for love—but for a variety of other reasons.

Some noticeable improvements have occurred. Spiritually, seven per cent of mainland Chinese now profess Christianity. Physically, transportation has greatly improved with the building of new bridges and railways. Culturally, during the Cultural Revolution, young people tried to destroy all religion, but China's youth of today will listen to the gospel.

In the early days under communism, the government dispersed some Christians to labour camps in remote areas in northwest China—areas historically Muslim. When the government told them to go and do as they liked, they did just that— they formed gospel bands based on those they had known earlier under the leadership of Paul's father and other evangelists. The next generation of Christians in the northwest have now begun contacting CNEC/Partners International.

Appendix 5: Dr. Allen B. Finley and Ruth Finley

Allen and Ruth Finley have known Paul Chang and his wife Nien-chang—and have remained close friends—since their early days with CNEC/Partners International (PI) in California.

***

Mission leaders have described the Reverend Dr. Allen B. Finley as, "A man on the cutting edge of missions." For 27 years he served as the international president of CNEC/PI. In his present position as senior associate with PI, Finley represents and speaks on behalf of PI in conferences and churches.

As a mission leader, Dr. Finley travelled nearly three million miles, visiting isolated jungle villages, planning with national boards and leaders, listening to nationals share their burdens and visions, and preaching in grass churches and urban edifices.

At home in almost any culture Finley brings with him the heart and passion for enabling the third-world church and an understanding of what the North American church needs to know in order to develop a balanced and meaningful missions program. He has spoken in missions conferences across the country and has participated in international conferences such as the World Evangelism Congress held in Berlin (1966),

Lausanne (1974), Pattaya, Thailand (1980), Amsterdam (1983), Mission "87" in Holland and AD 2000 in Singapore (1989).

Dr. Finley's early ministry included being a church pastor and serving a term as a missionary in Lebanon and Syria. He also spent seven years working as west-coast director for International Students Incorporated. He has written a number of papers and articles and has co-authored with Lorry Lutz a book on assisting nationals called *The Family Tie*. He has served as consultant to the U.S. Center for World Missions in Pasadena, California.

***

Ruth Finley has dedicated her entire adult life to working cross-culturally. As speaker-at-large for PI, she brings a lifetime of experiences and insights gained working with people of other cultures. Like her husband, she has broad experience and involvement with modern missionary development.

Having circled the globe many times over during 33 years with PI, she has frequently visited third-world leaders and their families, developing warm relationships with many of them. During the time her husband served as president, she directed sponsorship programs for PI.

An exciting dimension to Ruth's ministry has been to coordinate a mission curriculum project that has produced seven complete Sunday school curricula. She has watched children's interest in missions increase as they learn from these intriguing, suspense-filled true stories of children overseas.

Using costumes collected during her world travels, Ruth enjoys conducting an interesting *Parade of Nations* for churches and women's groups. Her narration gives a rich, cross-cultural world view with an emphasis on the unreached peoples of the world.

As an effective communicator, those organizing church mission conferences and other special meetings locally and around the world increasingly call on her as keynote speaker.

Appendix 6: Singapore Bible College

The Singapore Bible College has figured prominently in the life of Paul Chang and the work of CNEC in Southeast Asia. Its long history often interconnects and runs parallel with that of CNEC and Paul Chang.

Soon after Calvin Chao—an original CNEC worker and well known to Paul Chang in China—arrived from the Chinese mainland, he began working with the Singapore Inter-Church Union. He started a short-term Bible school which soon blossomed into a full-time institution. The Singapore Theological Seminary began on September 7, 1952 with nine students. CNEC helped with financial gifts and seconded personnel. The Overseas Missionary Fellowship brought in Chinese-speaking men and women with long experience in College work in China. The school received broad support and encouragement from the Christian community in Singapore and Southeast Asia.

In June of 1955 they held their first graduation. In 1956 the college became independent from the Inter-Church Union, developing into an autonomous institution.

In 1962 the Singapore Theological Seminary changed its name to the Singapore Bible College (SBC). Paul Chang became an active board member in 1974. In 1978 the Asia Theological Association accredited SBC to confer B.TH. degrees and diplomas in theology. In 1984 SBC's School of Graduate Studies began offering M.DIV., M.M.S., and M.C.S. degrees.

In 1983 Paul Chang accepted the challenge from Dr. Maak Hay Chun, then principal of SBC, to establish a School of Church Music at SBC. This so perfectly fitted Paul's training and interests that he threw himself into the task and remained active in the school as a faculty member and dean until 1991. The fact that information on SBC published in 1992 lists him as fulltime faculty, reflects the degree of Paul's commitment to the task. Throughout those years he maintained his full-time CNEC responsibilities.

From its inception until today the development of the SBC campus has kept pace with the requirements of a growing student body. From a temporary and borrowed building, it has grown into a modern campus.

Students from many denominational backgrounds attend the school and subsequently take ministry positions with a great variety of church and para-church organizations.

Appendix 7: Dr. Oswald Smith—The Peoples Church

During Dr. Oswald Smith's ministry as an evangelist, he held crusades world-wide, visiting more than 75 countries. As an author, he wrote 35 books which were translated into 118 languages. As a songwriter and poet, he wrote more than 1,200 gospel songs and poems. Among the best known of his songs are *The Glory of His Presence* and *Then Jesus Came*. Most people remember Smith for his establishment of The Peoples Church in Toronto and its subsequent missions program. He lent his expertise to other churches of many denominations to help establish mission conferences and programs for them.

He preached his first service at Peoples on September 9, 1928.

In 1959, Smith transferred the pastorate of The Peoples Church to his son, Paul B. Smith, while he retained such titles as founder, missionary pastor and pastor emeritus. Dr. Paul, born in Toronto in 1921, began preaching in 1940.

Oswald J. Smith died in 1986. Paul B. Smith died in the 90s.

The church continued its missions emphasis and in early 2003, supported 68 mission agencies, 325 missionaries, and 155 nationals.[1]

---

[1] Numbers from The Peoples Church web site: www.thepeopleschurch.ca

Appendix 8: Dr. Paul Chang's Music Philosophy

Challenges for Musicians in the Present Day, by Paul Chang

Every time I join the Lisu brothers and sisters of Myanmar in their worship I truly admire their singing. They sing almost any hymn in four-part a cappella. Their natural talent in being able to draw out such beautiful harmonies really touches one's heart. The rendering of Hallelujah Chorus, sung at the end of the service as a sacrifice of praise to God, was truly moving! All this makes me think of the contemporary praise and worship styles in churches today. Obviously, hymn-singing is gradually neglected. What takes its place is something that has no theme, subject, structure, direction, or objective. Even the melodies and rhythms contain "rock" elements. What's more, the worship teams appear like actors on stage with the worshippers like audiences. They use their hands more than their mouths in praising God. Though this does not include all praise and worship services, it is definitely the trend in today's worship culture.

For born-again Christians, God had granted us the right to use music to worship and to praise Him: this is church music. The music which believers offer to God is set apart as holy, revealed through the Holy Spirit. The Bible always reminds us that we are "a people who sing a new song," which is to say "He put a new song in my mouth, a hymn of praise to our God" (Psalm 40:3). "Sing joyfully to the Lord, you righteous; it is fitting for the upright to praise Him" (Psalm 30:1). In the book of Revelation, it is recorded that the twelve elders knelt down before the Lamb, and they sang a new song, "You are worthy to take the scroll and to open its seals because You were slain, and with Your blood You purchased men for God from every tribe and language and people and nation" (Rev. 5:8-9). It is evident that the music we use to worship God has to be set apart as holy, it is spiritual music.

First of all, the church musician must ensure that he or she has correct views of God and worship, as well as having a firm foundation of church music. It is through proper order of worship and strict adherence in selecting hymns that God's transcendence and imminence are revealed. Thus, worshippers will truly know the God they worship. In comparison a hurried worship flow will depict a God who lacks direction and goal; a worship team that lacks preparation will make people feel that our God is sluggish; choosing a song that lacks liveliness and artistry makes our God mechanical; whereas music that is empty of creativity will depict a dull God.

Since we are created in the image of God, and our lives have been moulded through Jesus Christ, we should manifest God's holiness, righteousness, loving kindness, mercy, omnipotence, authority, greatness, majesty and eternity through our worship. On the other hand, for the sake of the gospel, we should even more use music to tell the world about God's love, the Word became flesh, shed His blood, rose from the dead, gave people new lives, letting them become children of God, and his dwelling in their midst. Therefore, the challenges and responsibilities of church musicians today are to provide authentic worship and music so as to reveal God's image as Creator and Saviour in today's praise and worship culture.

Appendix 9: Dr. Charles (Chuck) Bennett

In 1968 Chuck Bennett began his missionary career as a pilot with Missionary Aviation Fellowship (MAF), flying for them in Mexico for 13 years. He next became MAF Director of Research and Evaluations, doing on-the-spot evaluations of about 40 client mission agencies in 20 countries. He became president of MAF in 1973, founded Air Serve International in 1984, and then accepted the position of president of Partners International in 1991. Following his retirement from PI in 2001, he joined Paraclete Mission Group as President and CEO.

Appendix 10: A Brief History of CNEC
Southeast Asia

1943

When Japan invaded China, many Western missionaries fled the country. After returning home, the Reverend Duncan McRoberts felt it was almost impossible to return to China as a missionary. But a possible way was to help the local Chinese Christians to evangelise their own people. Thereafter, a few Christian businessmen including Dr. N.A. Jepson established the Chinese Native Evangelistic Crusade. They invited the Reverend Calvin Chao to become first General Director and Doris Lim to become the first secretary. They started work in April 1943 from an office in Guizhou Province.

1944

The office and part of the staff moved to Chongqing city. During this time Rev. Chia Yu-ming helped to establish the Chongqing Bible Institute. CNEC aided more than ten Bible students to complete their studies. They published bulletins and sent preaching bands. They also established a Christian Fellowship for university students from all over China. Soon CNEC ministries started reaching inland provinces like Sichuan, Shanxi, Ganshu and Xinjiang.

1945

The war forced CNEC to move its office to Shanghai and build the Tai-tung Seminary in Nanjing with the Professor Chang Hsueh Kung as its first principal. They also began an orphanage in Nanjing. The Shanghai Bible Institute started with Rev. Alfred Chow as principal. Qianguang Bible Institute began in Guizhou.

1947

Rev. Calvin Chao resigned from office and the Rev. Alfred Chow replaced him. Fred Savage became treasurer and offered his own home—a three-storey building—as the CNEC office.

1949

The Reverends Alfred Chow and Fred Savage came to Hong Kong subsequently to establish an office. Shu Jen Jen and Yu Li-chan from Bethel Bible College joined CNEC to establish the Hong Kong Bible College (now the Bible Seminary of Hong Kong). Morning Light magazine began publishing and the Hong Kong Bible Laymen Training School also began this year. Bible students Yan Tong Mei from Shanghai, Paul Chang, son of Chang Hsueh-Kung and Chen Sing Ying from Sichuan fled communist China and joined CNEC in Hong Kong.

1950

Rev. Calvin Chao came back to Hong Kong and again took up the position of field director. Subsequently he went down to Southeast Asia to establish preaching points in Johor Bahru in Malaysia and Bangkok, Chiangrai, Chiengkham and Lamphang, in Thailand.

1951

Following the political upheaval in China, more CNEC ministries gradually relocated to Southeast Asia. Malaysia, which then included Singapore, was a major target for evangelization. During this year CNEC established a headquarters in Singapore. It was a strategic centre for thousands of Chinese people living in the region.

1952

The ministries in Singapore had spread out to seven new villages. Singapore Bible College (SBC)—then Singapore Theological Seminary—established under the leadership of Rev. Calvin Chao (acting principal). CNEC invited local people to form a board of directors for the school. CNEC financially aided three other lecturing couples, provided scholarships for five students, and helped to finance some miscellaneous expenses. They rented a place at 13 Ipoh Lane and began with the first batch of students numbering only seven. The need for mission workers to evangelize in Malaysia's new villages was pressing.

Mrs. Myrtle Tan responded promptly to the call. More workers joined later to build preaching points in Plentong, Pandan, Masai, Ulu Tiram, and elsewhere within Johore State. They preached the gospel among the rubber plantation workers; souls were saved and chapels built.

1954

Three workers were sent to Ipoh to start ministering to people in Berchem new village. The people responded to the gospel even more readily than those in Johor. Rev. Calvin Chao became the first Field Director of CNEC Southeast Asia. Following an agreement with the 7th District of the Church of Christ in Thailand, CNEC workers established the first church in Phitsunaloke.

1955

Ministries in Thailand grew very quickly. CNEC workers started a short-term Bible school in Bangkok and built chapels in Lamphang and Uttaragit.

1956

CNEC International President Mr. Cecil Kettle visited Southeast Asia this year. Rev. Calvin Chao resigned and emigrated to the United States. At this stage, CNEC workers established nine ministries in Southeast Asia with 20 full-time workers.

1957

Lorong Tai Seng Chapel (now Tai Seng Christian Church) was the first church established in Singapore. Fire destroyed Phitsunaloke Chapel. Rev. John Lu became the second Southeast Asia Field Director. Singapore Bible College moved to 1 Baker Road from Ipoh Lane. CNEC International's Crowell Foundation helped to purchase and renovate the new building. Rev. Yu Li-chan came to Singapore to lecture full-time at SBC.

1958

The Singapore Bible College purchased the present premises at 9-11 Adam Road and moved in gradually in October this year.

1959

CNEC first workers' retreat was held in the Singapore Bible College with Dr. Ray Stedman as the speaker. CNEC office moved from Sophia Road to Branksome Road in Katong. Five full-time workers joined the ranks. Bartley Road Christian Church Chinese ministry started in a home by Bible students Calvin Tan Tsong Hua and Zhao Pan Wen while Jacob Fung was the pastor. Rev. John Lu baptised the first batch of 13 converts on April 11.

1960

Mrs. Myrtle Tan established the third chapel in Singapore at Sembawang. Rev. Allen Finley became General Director of CNEC International. In October he visited Southeast Asia. CNEC established a field office in Johor Bahru, Malaysia. Johor Bahru Church began with 15 Sunday school students. Christians from the burned-down Phitsunaloke Chapel bought another block of land to rebuild their church. Bangkok's short term Bible school had now increased to three hundred students.

1961

Doris, the beloved wife of our Field Director, Rev. John Lu, went home to be with the Lord this year. Singapore field office moved from Branksome Road to Eastern Mansion.

1962

Mr. & Mrs. Loo Soon Fun, workers in Ipoh were killed in a car accident. Our hearts deeply grieved. They left behind four orphans. Rev. John Lu married Jessie Chock Man. Woodland Chapel in Singapore began near the Malaysian border. The English ministry of Bartley Road Christian Church began in August.

1963

Penang Church in Malaysia established. Rev. Chen Sing Ying and family came from Hong Kong and established the Short-Term Laymen's Bible School in Singapore.

1964

Field office moved in to Jalan Jelita near Holland Road in August and dedicated one of the buildings to the memory of the late Mrs. Doris Lu and Miss M. Allitt of Australia.

1965

Chiangrai Church in Thailand bought a piece of land and built their own church after two years of renting other premises. Rev. and Mrs. John Lu went overseas for deputation work. CNEC Southeast Asia set up an executive committee with seven members and elected Vun Kyn Hee as chairman.

1966

Rev. John Lu returned to Singapore. World Wide Christian Literature Crusade and CNEC sought co-operation to start literature ministry in Singapore.

1967

The Reverend and Mrs. Paul Chang visited Singapore and took part in a musical evangelistic rally. Chiengkham Christian Church officially opened on March 27. MacPherson Christian Church began operation in MacPherson Housing Estate.

1968

North Borneo mission joined CNEC and began operating in Sarawak, East Malaysia. Rev. A. Finley, Rev. Wilson, and Mrs. N.A. Jepson (wife of CNEC founder) visited Southeast Asia mission field.

1969

Miss F.M. Cook, chairman of CNEC Australian Council visited Singapore's headquarters. Living Water Christian Church started operating in Toa Payoh Housing Estate.

1970
Co-worker Wang Chiau Lin retired from his ministries in Penang Christian Church. Field Director Rev. John Lu retired and emigrated to Australia in August. Lamphang Church dedicated its new chapel. Rev. Arthur Gee and family came from USA to succeed Rev. John Lu as Southeast Asia Field Director. Toa Payoh Bible Church started its ministries in Toa Payoh East Housing Estate.

1971
Registration of CNEC in Malaysia received approval. Ministries began in West Kalimantan, and workers established Hwei Hai Chapel in North Thailand. CNEC and Overseas Crusade sought cooperation in publishing Good News Bilingual Correspondence Course. Pastor Daniel Tan was ordained minister in Johor Bahru.

1972
Mr. Yap Fui Chung dedicated his house for the Lord's use. This move prompted the establishment of the True Blessing Church. Sembawang Grace Chapel in Singapore began operation. Sanggau's Antioch Church and Macedonian Chapel began in West Kalimantan. CNEC churches ordained Pastor John Cheong as a minister in Singapore.

1973
Ipoh Faith Christian Church reached out to the Indian Community. Johor Bahru Church converted a supermarket into a chapel and CNEC's field office relocated there. Brighton Chapel (now affiliated with Bartley Church) began in Singapore. OMF transferred the management and care of Triang Chapel in Pahang state to CNEC. CNEC organised a first-ever athletic meeting for churches in Singapore.

1974
After 20 years serving in CNEC, Sister Yow Choy Ley retired.

Tape Inspiration Lending Library began operation. Segamat
Chapel became a para-church of Johor Bahru Church. Rev.
Arthur Gee returned to the US for deputation work while Rev.
Paul Chang came to act as interim field director. The churches
ordained Pastors Anthony Ang, Paul Huang, Peter Pan and
James Tjondro as ministers

1975
Jerantut Chapel in Pahang joined CNEC. CNEC ministries started
in Jakarta, Indonesia.

1976
Sponsor-a-Child program (SAC) started in North Thailand to
help the underprivileged children attend schools, helping 75
children in Hwei Ph'ng village. A student ministry began in
Petaling Jaya, adjacent to Kuala Lumpur. The Tape Lending
Library produced six message master tapes for CCCOWE Rev.
Chiang Wei Sin and Dr. Maak Hay Chun taped the first series
of *Christian Ethics* and *Tape Evangelism* in Mandarin. CNEC
Southeast Asia celebrated its 25th anniversary at Tao Payoh
Methodist Church. On the same day Pastors Matthew Ding and
Calvin Tan were ordained as ministers. A project to purchase a
new office site for Singapore Field Office was initiated.

1977
CNEC established a preaching point in Kemayan, Malaysia and
established Galilee Church, Pontianak. CNEC set up an office in
Pontianak, West Kalimantan, after purchasing a three-storey
building. Under the leadership of Rev. Paul Huang, Chiangrai
Church completed a new building. Rev. Huang also directed the
overall ministries in North Thailand and churches in the mountainous areas. CNEC bought the 134-136 Braddell Road premises
and gained approval for office and church use. The bilingual
Hymns of Praise was ready for publication. Sister Hannah Koh
and Tom Lim from Hong Kong assisted in the final phase of
compilation. Rev. Arthur Gee was transferred to Hong Kong to
be the East Asia Field Director while Rev. Paul Chang took up

the position of Director for South East Asia.

1978
Reverend Matthew Ding established Glory Joy Christian Church and began ministering in the Upper Thomson area. Rev. Chen Sing Ying retired after 16 years of service in Bible Laymen Training School.

1979
Rev. Joshua Chiu of Eng Kong Church in Singapore went home to be with the Lord on February 6. Pastor Luke Goh of Johor Bahru Vision Church was ordained a minister on November 20. Rev. Paul Chang and Rev. Yan Ta Ann of Lashio, Myanmar, contemplating a joint venture for Burmese ministries. Five hundred Dayaks gathered for the first time in a three-day gospel camp in Empaong, West Kalimantan.

1981
Twelve hundred children from North Thailand and West Kalimantan enrolled into the SAC program. Northern Burma Bible Institute commenced in July. Bartley Christian Church completed its new building located in How Sun Drive in February. Pastor Daniel Lee and family came to Singapore from Hong Kong in December to minister in Tai Seng Christian Church. Johor Bahru Vision Church planted a daughter church, Christian Gospel Centre in Skudai. The pastor is Foo Swee Sang. Each month the Tape Lending Library lent out about one hundred tapes in five different dialects under the title *Basic Christianity*.

1983
The churches ordained Pastor Daniel Lee as a minister on January 23. Penang Christian Church bought a new building and changed its name to Christ's Commission Centre. Chiengkham Church began a new work in Yun Hua village, north Thailand.

1984

Sister Lee Sue Eng of Kemayan Church offered a piece of land of her own for church use. Through the corporate effort of the church members, a new church building was built. MacPherson Church rented a terrace house at Jalan Lunder Kuda in Johor Bahru to establish a preaching point. Initially 20 people attended the services. Toa Payoh Bible Church pastor Joseph Yap and wife Lynelle went to Liberia to be missionaries at Monrovia. Under the SAC program, Setia Bakti Secondary School was established in a Dyak village in West Kalimantan. Pastor Chang Wen Chye began gospel work in Ban Hin Teck (now Theod Thai), north Thailand.

1985

Pastor Emeritus John Willis of Bartley Christian Church celebrated his 80th birthday on November 18. Proceeds of cash gifts were dedicated to the Singapore Bible College, John Willis Scholarship Fund. Pastor David Soo reported that 22 Akha families living in Hwei Mei Lin have become Christians. Hwei Hai Bible Institute commenced on May 20 with 28 students. The first principal was Rev. Li Lap Wai.

1986

Pastor James Lai was ordained a minister on March 2. CNEC held a thanksgiving service for its 35th anniversary at Newton Life Church. Rev. Kao Yun Han from Canada spoke at the meeting. Glory Joy Christian Church bought a detached house in Sembawang and started gathering there. Pastor and Mrs. Raymond Ho from Malaysia went to serve in Pontianak and make plans to establish a training centre. Pastor Boonprasert Vijitrakul ventured to begin the first urban outreach in Chiangmai.

1987

Pastor Foo Swee Sang from Skudai was ordained a minister on May 18. Rev. and Mrs. Phun Duma, Burmese nationals, began new village ministries among the Chin tribe. They started the

Kulai Vision Church after a series of gospel meetings in that area. The main workers were Rev. Foo Swee Sang, Pastor Chan Hin Kee, and Pastor Chok Kim Sin. The name was changed to Evangel Christian Church and the total membership increased to over 60. Rev. Yan Ta Ann led a gospel team to Kutkai in Burma and preached to three thousand people there. Triang Christian Church initiated a plan to build a new church building. A mini theological seminary began in Pontianak in August. They initially had 20 students.

1988

Tai Seng Christian Church in Singapore bought a church building at 140 Yio Chu Kang Road in November. CNEC and the 12th District Churches in north Thailand combined and held a retreat for local church leaders. Dr. Maak Hay Chun and Elder Wu Yong were speakers. Two of the 12 churches supported by CNEC in north Thailand have become self-supporting. The gospel has reached the surrounding tribal peoples such as the Lahu, Akha, and Lisu. Fifteen graduates from the Hwei Hai Bible Institute went to the nearby villages to preach the gospel. CNEC in West Kalimantan sent and supported 28 pastors (7 Chinese, 16 Dayaks, 4 Javanese and 1 Indonesian) to pastor 30 local churches there.

1989

Christians from CNEC churches who worked or studied in Kuala Lumpur discussed with the Reverends Luke Goh and James Lai about founding a Chinese church in that area. Christian Fellowship Centre was set up in July with Sister Chua Sui Kheng as the evangelist. The Tamil Evangelical Christian Church began its ministries among Tamil-speaking Indians in Rantau Negeri Sembilan. The "Gospel Cow" project began in October in Lao Liu Zai to assist poor Christian families and to help churches become self-supporting. Galilee Church in Pontian bought a two-storey building on September 22 to cater to church ministry expansion. Hwei Ma Ern Chapel began in north Thailand in April. Antioch Church in Sanggau started building a student centre in July.

1990

Toa Payoh Bible Church (now The People's Bible Church and Logos Christian Church) completed its five-storey building at Lorong Ah Soo in March. Dedication service was held on April 27. Logos Christian Church began grassroots ministry with Bethlehem Sunday Evening Worship Service in September. Johor Bahru Vision Church planted another church at Johor Jaya, a new housing estate, with Lim Jiun Dien as the pastor. Pastor Yeoh Kok Lee was ordained a minister on August 20.

1991

On January 1 Pastor Tham Kwok Wah started Kim Keat Christian Church using the former premises of Toa Payoh Bible Church. The church aims to reach out to the many new residents and young families in the area. God provided a two-storey semi-detached house for Evangel Christian Church in Johor Bahru for meetings after the rent contract for the previous premises expired. Christian Gospel Centre in Skudai, Johor, bought a two-storey shop-house for church gatherings. Bartley Christian Church started a daughter church at Pasir Ris Housing Estate in August.

1992

Pastor and Mrs. Cha Tan Yone launched a "Grace Haven" that adopted four orphans initially in Myanmar. Chinese Christian Bible Institute (formerly Northern Burma Bible College) relocated to Maymyo in July. The Good News Correspondence Course office shifted to the Malaysian Field Office in Johor Bahru for the convenience of students. Partners Training Centre in Skudai began under the leadership of Rev. James Lai and Pastor Lim San Yang. The purpose of the ministry was to train Christians for church services and evangelism. Pastor Boonprasert of Blessing Church in Chiangmai was ordained a minister on March 7. CNEC formed a new executive committee in April for north Thailand ministries under the leadership of

Rev. Boonprasert. Workmen completed the expansion and renovation work of the CNEC headquarters and Neighbourhood Church.

1993
The Reverends Paul Chang and Arthur Gee and Dr. William Ho visited churches and co-workers in areas near the Thailand/Myanmar border during a two-week Bible training session in January. Grace Haven in Myanmar became incorporated under government law—adopted orphans have increased to 27. CNEC Southeast Asia celebrated its 50th anniversary on July 10 with a thanksgiving service at The People's Bible Church. Construction completed and dedication held for the Chiangmai Evangelism Centre in north Thailand. This four-storey building houses the Chiangmai Blessings Church, CNEC Chiangmai office, with facilities for outreach and training.

1994
Rev. Joseph Ting Ming Kion of True Blessing Church in Johor Baru, Malaysia went home to be with the Lord after a long battle with liver cancer. His wife, Pastor Chan Lai Chu, takes over. Pastor Sylvia Ooi Wan Sheng of Logos Christian Church re-edited *Hymns of Praise*. The original 470 songs remain, and the new edition includes new Scripture verses for responsive reading and prayers.

1995
A dedication service was held for the new office of CNEC Malaysia. The staff moved in December last year. Dedication held for the new building for Grace Haven in Lashio, Myanmar. Rev. Paul Chang officiated; Dr Ben Sia and Rev. Nigel Lau from Australia attended along with about seven hundred local people. The number of children at the orphanage has increased to one hundred, twenty from eight minority tribes.

1996
The New Vision drug rehabilitation centre established near

Chiangmai, Thailand.

1997

CNEC Malaysia sent co-worker Pastor Charles Sundram to reach the Orang Laut people (Sea Dayaks) along the eastern shores of Johor. The second Grace Haven established under the leadership of Yi Zhan Cheng in Lao Jie, Myanmar, near the border with Yunnan province of China. At about the same time, God opened a third door for a similar ministry in Nanpaka, a town in the mountainous district of Nan Kan, near the China border and west of Lao Jie.

1998

Construction completed for Holy Light Chapel in Lashio, Myanmar, and begins for the Geng-Yun student centre in Chiangrai, Thailand. Rev. Phun Duma and Khuang Nawni established Bethel Home in Yangon, Myanmar. Also CNEC workers established Putra Christian Center in Selangor and Vision Church in Taman Perling, Johor, Malaysia. CNEC West Kalimantan occupied a new building in Pontianak. The ETSI mini-seminary moved into the old CNEC office.

1999

Construction completed for Geng-Yun student centre in Chiangrai. New Vision drug rehabilitation centre in Chiangmai plans a new ministry for female drug addicts. Paul Chang, Chuck Bennett, Cha Tan Yone and Chiang Ho Heng (Henry) were involved in a car accident in the mountains of northern Myanmar. Their vehicle collided head-on with an on-coming truck. The four sustained various injuries. God spared their lives and provided help through a stranger. CNEC started a new ministry in Mei He, Myanmar—an orchard-cum-drug rehab centre, on a 20-acre piece of land. The International Council admitted the CNEC-SEA office in Singapore as an affiliate council, joining the CNEC/PI Alliance which includes councils from the United States, the United Kingdom, Canada, Australia, and Japan. The Crossroads Centre in Phnom Penh, Cambodia opened, with 12 young men who were university students under the leadership of Rev. Wati Longkumer, a missionary from Nagaland, India.

2000
Gereja Kristen Nasional Injili (GKNI) in West Kalimantan registered with Indonesia's Department of Religion. This enables GNIK to do evangelism and plant churches. CNEC organized its first Chinese missions conference with its eight affiliated Chinese churches on Aug 25 to 27, at the Logos Christian Church. Rev. Samuel Chu, principal of the Hong Kong Bible Seminary was keynote speaker. Construction began on Filipi Centre in Sekadau, West Kalimantan. This centre aims to help orphans and children from needy families in the area. CNEC launched the micro-enterprises program. This poverty-alleviation program offers small interest-free loans to help churches and poor members start small businesses or income-generating farming projects in order to become economically productive and financially self-supporting.

2001
Inauguration service held for the Filipi Centre in Sekadau, West Kalimantan. It started with 15 orphans. Co-workers and government officials attended. One official stated that Filipi Centre is the very first orphanage in Sanggau province of West Kalimantan, and one run by Christians. The women's department of New Vision drug rehabilitation centre launched and soon reached full accommodation (8–10). A missionary couple, David Ooi and Moonjung Nam, took over the ministry of the Crossroads Centre in Phnom Penh, Cambodia, replacing Rev. Wati.

2002
Kim Keat Christian Church held a church building dedication service at its new church premises at 11 Beng Wan Road in Singapore. Living Streams Christian Church purchased its own building at 56/56A Boundary Road, after many years of renting a public housing flat in Toa Payoh, Singapore. Crossroads min-

istry in Phnom Penh took in its first batch of four female university students. The dorm for female students is a rented building a short distance away from the first building. CNEC Singapore published David Soo book, *A Most Unlikely Evangelist*. From a print run of one thousand, CNEC Australia took more than seven hundred copies as gifts for donors who contributed to the north Thailand tribal ministry. CNEC established a Student Centre in Mandalay, Myanmar along the line of Crossroads Centre in Phnom Penh—a bridging ministry to provide dormitory, training and church in the Mandalay area. The dorm will accept high school and university students.[95]

NOTES

1. Known in English as Confucius—551–479 BC.

2. Genesis 1:1.

3. John 1:1.

4. Also known as the Hwang Ho or Yellow River.

5. For a chart of Chinese Dynasties and history, see Appendix 1.

6. The doctrine that kings derive their authority from God, not from their subjects.

7. The 19th century political doctrine that the United States must expand westward to the Pacific and exert economic and social control over North America.

8. Page XVIII, Stursberg, *No Foreign Bones in China*.

9. This German concession or sphere of influence began in 1896 when the Germans seized the ports of Qingdao and Kiaochow following the murder of two German priests.

10. Paul Chang watched one of those massacres from an attic window.

11. Page 194, Stursberg, *No Foreign Bones in China*.

12. Acts 1:8

13. See Wiseman, *Disciples of Joy*, pp. 40, 41.

14. Page 31, Outerbridge, *Lost Churches of China*.

15. Page 43–48, Outerbridge, *Lost Churches of China*.

16. Page 712, Wells, *The Outline of History*.

17. Page 67, Outerbridge, *Lost Churches of China*.

18. Ralph R. Covell "Trickle Down Evangelism," *Christianity Today/Christian History Magazine*, Issue 52, Vol. XV, No. 4. P. 24.

19. Page 120, Outerbridge, citing Gustav Warneck, *Lost Churches of China.*

20. Pages xc, xci, Stauffer, *The Christian Occupation of China.*

21. Paul Chang was also born in Shandong province.

22. Two great philosophers of the West, Socrates and Aristotle, lived only a short time later.

23. As quoted in the web site:
http://religion-cults.com/Eastern/Confucianism/confuci.htm

24. In Chinese Shandong means, "East of the Mountains." You will find many alternate spellings: Shandung, Shantung, Shantong. Chang Bao-wha (Paul Chang) was born in the city of Teng-xian, now known by its modern name, Tseng Cha.

25. Each generation had a different designation. All of Chang Hsueh Kung's children bore the prefix *Bao* as part of their given names.

26. Hung Dai-wei became a medical doctor. Dei-wei is the Mandarin version of the biblical name David.

27. The Internet abounds with well-documented web sites that graphi-cally illustrate the atrocities committed by the Japanese Imperial Army during that time.

28. Because of the international dateline, the raid on Pearl Harbour occurred on December 7 in the Western world, but on December 8 in the East.

29. From the Web pages of CNEC/Partners International in Singapore– http://home.pacific.net.sg/~cnecsea/history.htm

30. In 1927 Chiang had married Soong Mei-ling—a graduate of Wellesley College, Boston—and converted to Christianity.

31. Now known as Biola University.

32. The China Inland Mission is now known as the Overseas Missionary Fellowship.

33. Hebrews 12:12.

34. II Timothy 4:17.

35. In an attempt to control the Christian Church, the government created the Three-Self Patriotic Movement. Only pastors or workers registered with it receive government recognition. Although not originally envisioned as a denomination, it now functions as such.

36. The school now uses the name Seattle Pacific University.

37. Today, CNEC/Partners International will continue support to national workers who have served with a partner ministry and wish to take a study break overseas for advanced studies.

38. This church still financially supports the Changs.

39. Why Mark? In the Bible Mark was the spiritual son of the Apostle Paul. They also gave him the Chinese names of Zhong Guang. *Zhong* means loyal; *Guang* means light.

40. Fred Manning had worked as a home missionary in the West Virginia mountains. When he retired in 1965 at age 65, he joined CNEC as a volunteer representative. He served in that capacity for 22 years, contacting thousands of churches all over the southern states, resulting in financial support for a multitude of national Christian workers and sponsored children.

41. Those churches later became part of a fast-growing denomination now known as the Presbyterian Church in America (PCA).

42. At the time of writing, seven of the PCA churches contacted on that tour still regularly support Paul Chang and the work of Partners International.

43. 2.5 pounds equals 1.3 kilograms.

44. They named her after Ruth Finley. They also gave her the Chinese name of Xian Guang. *Xian* speaks of grace or beauty; *Guang* means light.

45. Oswald J Smith, *The Challenge of Missions*, (Burlington, Ontario). Welch, 1984. See Appendix 9 for more information on The Peoples Church, Toronto.

46. John Kao deserves special mention. Like Paul Chang, he dedicated his life to the work of CNEC and the evangelization of the Chinese community. His story appears in Appendix 2.

47. Page 4, Wiltshire, *Last Prize of the Empire*.

48. An age-old custom of trying to buy offices or favour in the church—named for the Simon of Acts 8:9–24 who tried to buy spiritual gifts from the apostles.

49. A young man, Ng Wei Sim, evangelized through the basketball ministry, later became the pastor of a branch of the CNEC Fellowship Church. Two other young men also went to seminary and became pastors, one in Sydney, Australia, and the other in Hong Kong.

50. Cheung and Chang are variant spellings of the same family name—Cheung being the Cantonese pronunciation and Chang Mandarin.

51. Simon and Esther later moved to California. Simon became a pastor and Esther worked with the American CNEC council as a fundraiser among Chinese Churches.

52. For information on the Lauzanne Conference and Covenant visit the web site: http://www.gospelcom.net/lcwe/story.html

53. Kalimantan is the Indonesian-ruled portion of the island formerly called Borneo.

54. Pages 805, 806, Dalton, *Indonesian Handbook*.

55. *I Cannot Dream Less* by Ray Wiseman tells the story of Dr. Marantika's church-planting seminary.

56. For this amazing story, read *Disciples of Joy* by Ray Wiseman.

57. Acts 1:8.

58. Matthew 8:20.

59. Harold Stevens had worked for many years with Africa Evangelical Fellowship (now part of SIM). In the mid-1970s he left that field and accepted a position as a representative with CNEC raising funds to support national workers.

60. Produced in an age when many Christian organizations showed little interest in copyright, CNEC Singapore obtained copyright permission through Zondervan's Singspiration division on hymns not in the public domain. In 1995 and 1996, with some changes in the editorial committee, they reedited and reissued the book. In the process they added responsive readings, calls to worship, and benedictions in both Chinese and English. *Hymns of Praise* marks an important accomplishment in Paul's career—in 1992 Biola University in La Mirada (near Los Angeles), California, conferred an honourary doctorate on him (D.LITT.) in recognition of his work on the hymnbook.

61. Isaiah 52:4.

62. See Appendix 3 for a short biography of David Soo.

63. In fact Boonprasert twice travelled to Singapore to take a one-year course at the Singapore Bible College—first in 1981 and again in 1984. Because he had been educated in the Thai language, he needed additional training in the Mandarin dialect to enhance his ministry among Chinese people. In Singapore he got to know the staff and ministries of the Southeast Asia CNEC office and worked in one of the local CNEC churches. During his second time there he met Khoo Boon Har, a Malaysian Chinese, and realized he had found his life companion.

64. Phil Dempster worked for the United States office of CNEC from 1976 to 1986—they later changed the name to Partners International (PI). He returned to Canada and joined the PI International board and the Canadian board in 1987. He became chairman of the PI International board in 1995 and the Canadian board in 1996.

65. Six-foot, four-inch.

66. Lily's story doesn't end there. When the civil war in Liberia drove them out, Lily and her husband looked elsewhere. At the time of writing Lily is a PH.D. student at Wheaton College while her husband studies at Trinity Divinity School. They have three children.

67. Bao-wen later headed China's most prestigious English-language training school, teaching English to diplomats and tourist guides.

68. The Apostle faced no personal problem with this issue—he preferred the single state but conceded that men and women might marry. See 1 Cor. Chapter 7, specifically verses 6 and 7.

69. Page 15, Buck, *My Several Worlds*.

70. Lorry and her husband worked in South Africa for many years, before turning their ministry, Youth Alive, over to African leadership. Back in the States they began working for CNEC. Lorry has written a number of books about support of national workers, including *The Family Tie*, coauthored with Allen Finley. The author has based some of the material concerning Paul's visits to China on that book.

71. The Apostle Paul could not always remember those he baptized (1 Cor. 1:15–16). Paul Chang is equally uncertain of names and numbers.

72. The story didn't end there. Paul later confronted the Chinese government, challenging the officials with: "You condemned a good man." The next year they released a statement erasing his father's condemnation and restoring his citizenship. This also removed the stigma from family members, making life easier for them.

73. For more information on SBC see indexes 6 and 7.

74. Isaiah 54:2,3.

75. The country formerly known as Burma.

76. Chuck Bennett served as International President of Partners International from 1991 through 1999. See a brief biography in Appendix 8.

77. Page 69–70 Bennett, *God in the Corners*.

78. Adapted from a special report dated June 1976.

79. Edited from a "Special Report from Paul Chang" dated June 1996.

80. Adapted from an article by Paul Chang in the CNEC Southeast Asia newsletter, *Praise and Prayer*, 1st quarter 2003.

81. We have changed the name and created some details based on reports by police and others who traced her to Bangkok. "Martha" belongs to the Lisu tribe, a people who typically use biblical names.

82. From an undated report entitled "Micro-Enterprise Project."

83. In North America we would call it a condominium.

84. From a prayer letter dated December, 1994.

85. From a prayer letter dated September 10, 1996.

86. When word of the success of the drug rehabilitation centre became known, the Myanmar government ordered it closed for a perceived "registration" violation. Workers in Myanmar have now found ways to restart the program.

87. Adapted from *Praise & Prayer*, July/August 1999.

88. In Southeast Asia people refer to small mobile telephones as hand phones.

89. From *Praise & Prayer*, July/August 1996.

90. Adapted from *Praise & Prayer*, Third Quarter, 2001.

91. Adapted from a column by Ray Wiseman that appeared in the *Guelph Mercury*, January 18, 2002.

92. 1 Timothy 3:1

93. Years ago, long before this author could even imagine the heady responsibility of writing the biographies of such great Christian leaders as Chris Marantika, Anand Chaudhari, or Paul Chang—indeed long before he dreamed of becoming a writer—he read this life-changing book.

94. We have gleaned and adapted information for this section from the annual reports submitted for the year 2002, from a variety of newsletters written during 2003, and from the staff in the CNEC/SEA office.

95. Adapted from a 50th anniversary booklet produced by CNEC Singapore with additional material provided by the Singapore office.

BIBLIOGRAPHY

Bennett, Chuck. *God in the Corners*. San Jose, California: Partners International-USA, 1997

Buck, Pearl S. *My Several Worlds*. Markham: Simon & Schuster of Canada, 1975.

Dalton, Bill. *Indonesia Handbook*. Chico (California): Moon Publications, 1988.

Drane, John (Editor). *Nelson's Illustrated Encyclopedia of the Bible*. Nashville: Thomas Nelson Inc., 2001.

Finley, Allen; Lutz, Lorry. *The Family Tie*. Nashville: Thomas Nelson Publishers, 1983.

Fraser, John. *The Chinese, Portrait of a People*. Toronto: Totem Books, 1981.

Hallesby, O. *Temperament and the Christian Faith*. Minneapolis: Augsburger Publishing House, 1962

Michael, Franz. *The Taiping Rebellion: History and Documents, vol. 2, Documents and Comments*. Seattle: University of Washington Press, 1971.

Museum of the Former Residence of Dr. Sun Yat-sen (The). *Sun Yat-Sen & Cui Heng*. Hong Kong: Urban Media Ltd, 1991.

McGlynn, Hilary (Editorial Director). T*he Hutchinson Pocket World Atlas*, Oxford: Helicon Publishing Ltd, 2001

Nida, Eugene A. *Customs and Cultures*. New York: Harper & Row, 1954.

Nida, Eugene A. *God's Word in Man's Language*. New York: Harper & Brothers, 1952.

Nida, Eugene A. *Religion Across Culture*. New York: Harper & Row, 1968.

Outerbridge, Leonard M. *The Lost Churches of China*. Philadelphia: The Westminister Press, 1952.

Rothwell, Joan. *A most Unlikely Evangelist*. Singapore: CNEC Southeast Asia, 2002.

Samagalski, Alan; Strauss, Robert; Buckley, Michael. *China a Travel Survival Kit*. Victoria (Australia): Lonely Planet Publications, 1988.

Sivin, Nathan; Wood, Frances; Brooke, Penny; Colin Ronan (Marshal Editions Limited - Editorial board). *The Contemporary Atlas of China*. London: Weidenfeld and Nicolson, 1988.

Stauffer, Milton T. (Editor). *The Christian Occupation of China*. Shanghai: China Continuation Committee, 1922.

Stursberg, Peter. *No Foreign Bones in China*. Edmonton: The University of Alberta Press, 2002

Wells, H.G. *The Outline of History*. Garden City, New York: Garden City Books, 1949.

Wen, Chihua. *The Red Mirror*. San Francisco: Westview Press, 1995.

Wiltshire, Trea. *Hong Kong, Last Prize of the Empire*. Hong Kong: FormAsia Books Limited, 1993

Wilkinson, Benjamin (Editor). *Let's go Southeast Asia*. New York: St. Martins Press, 1999.

Wiseman, Ray. *Disciples of Joy*. Brampton: Partners International-Canada, 1998

Wiseman, Ray. *I Cannot Dream Less*. Brampton: Partners International-Canada, 1993

INDEX

Some entries may refer to the related end note rather than the text on the page indicated.